Parapsychology
A Beginner's Guide

ONEWORLD BEGINNER'S GUIDES combine an original, inventive, and engaging approach with expert analysis on subjects ranging from art and history to religion and politics, and everything in-between. Innovative and affordable, books in the series are perfect for anyone curious about the way the world works and the big ideas of our time.

Beginners
GUIDES

Parapsychology
A Beginner's Guide

Dr Caroline Watt

ONEWORLD

A Oneworld Paperback Original

Published in North America, Great Britain and Australia by
Oneworld Publications, 2016
Reprinted, 2021, 2022

ISBN 978-1-78074-887-0
eISBN 978-1-78074-888-7

Typeset by Jayvee, Trivandrum, India
Printed and bound in Great Britain by Clays Ltd, Elcograf S.p.A.

Oneworld Publications
10 Bloomsbury Street
London, WC1B 3SR
England

Stay up to date with the latest books,
special offers, and exclusive content from
Oneworld with our newsletter

Sign up on our website
oneworld-publications.com

To my parents, David and Dorothy Dow

Contents

Acknowledgements

I am grateful to Mike Harpley and Shadi Doostdar at Oneworld for their encouragement and editorial guidance. I thank Professor Etzel Cardeña, Professor Adrian Parker, and Dr David Luke for giving valuable feedback on the draft manuscript. Professor Bernard Carr advised me on theoretical physics matters, for which I am very grateful. All along the way, I received vital help and support from my long-time collaborator and partner, Professor Richard Wiseman. Thanks Richard. Finally, I was fortunate to be awarded the Perrott-Warrick Senior Researcher Fellowship, which relieved me of some other academic duties so that I could devote time to writing this book, and I am deeply grateful for this support.

Terminology and phenomena

Parapsychologists study a wide range of paranormal experiences. The fictional Sue (in the USA) and her brother Jon (in Australia) will help to illustrate the categorization and terminology that parapsychologists tend to employ. A wider range of terms and acronyms is presented in the Glossary at the end of this book.

Extrasensory perception (ESP)

Work into ESP involves the following three topics:

Telepathy: The transfer of information between individuals by means other than the known senses (from the Ancient Greek word τῆλε or *tele*, meaning 'distant', and πάθος or *pathos*, meaning 'feeling'), e.g. Jon has a car accident and thinks about Sue. At the same time, Sue hears an internal voice 'telling' her that Jon has been involved in a car accident.

Precognition: The perception of information about future events, also referred to as future sight, second sight, and prophesy (from the Latin word *præ-*, meaning 'before', and *cognitio*, meaning 'acquiring knowledge'), e.g. Sue dreams that Jon will have a car accident, and just a day later he has a car accident.

Clairvoyance: The obtaining of information about a place or event by unknown means (from French words *clair*, meaning 'clear', and *voyance*, meaning 'vision'), e.g. Sue has no prior knowledge of the street where Jon is living, but one day she receives a vivid impression that he lives next to an unusual domed structure. Parapsychologists sometimes use the term 'remote viewing' to refer to instances of clairvoyance in which information is acquired from a geographical location.

Psychokinesis (PK)

The influence of mind on an object, physical system, or biological system, without physical interaction (from the Greek ψυχή or *psyche*, meaning 'mind', and κίνησις, meaning 'movement'). Abbreviated as PK, this work involves the following three topics:

Macro-PK: The large-scale movement of physical objects with the mind, sometimes referred to as 'telekinesis', e.g. Sue went to a dinner party where her friends started to mimic the feats of Uri Geller. Sue watched while a spoon held by her friend appeared to bend without any physical force being exerted.

Micro-PK: Mental influence over small-scale physical systems, such as dice and electronic random number generators, only detectable using statistics, e.g. Sue consistently beats the odds when she plays casino games involving dice.

Bio-PK: Mental influence over biological systems, including plants, insects and animals, in vitro samples, and humans. This category of research includes remote staring detection and distant healing, e.g. Jon is sitting on a bus. The hairs tingle on the back of his neck and he feels that he is being watched. When he looks around he sees that someone at the back of the bus is staring at him.

PSI

Often it is difficult in practice to distinguish between the above categories. For example, if Sue somehow detected that Jon's car had a mechanical fault, this might have caused unconscious anxiety that led to the dream. In this case, Sue may have been responding to information about the car's current danger-ous condition (= clairvoyance) rather than to future events (= precognition). Therefore, parapsychologists often use the neutral umbrella term 'psi' (rhymes with 'eye') to denote the unknown factor underlying both ESP and PK phenomena.

List of illustrations

The concrete evidence for most of the 'psychic' phenomena under discussion is good enough to hang a man twenty times over.

William James

Many brilliant men have investigated the paranormal but they have yet to find a single person who can, without trickery, send or receive even a three-letter word under test conditions.

Milbourne Christopher

1

Introduction: The roots of parapsychology

Surveys suggest that around 50% of those in both America and Britain believe in the existence of the paranormal, and about 30% of people claim to have had a psychic experience. This statistic means that, if you have not had a paranormal experience yourself, you probably know someone who has. This book describes the research that has been conducted in an attempt to understand these unusual, but surprisingly common, experiences.

The study of such experiences, parapsychology, can be traced back to some strange events in the mid-nineteenth century in Hydesville, New York, which seemed to suggest that some individuals could communicate with the deceased. Pioneering researchers grappled with the challenge of testing claims of afterlife communication. In the process they developed the three main approaches that are now employed in parapsychological research. But before we find out more about how parapsychology came to be what it is today, let's briefly consider what parapsychology is *not*.

Misconceptions about parapsychology

When I am sitting on an aeroplane and the stranger in the seat next to me asks what I do, I sometimes hesitate to answer. Yes, I am

a researcher looking at quite a fascinating and sometimes controversial topic. But before I tell my fellow traveller what my job
entails, I often have to dispel some myths that exist about parapsychology. For example, quite understandably, many people
associate parapsychology with popular films such as *Ghostbusters*.
In fact, parapsychologists do not run around in boiler suits, hunting down marauding ghosts with proton packs. Instead, like
other scientists, parapsychologists often carry out well-controlled
studies and publish their findings in both mainstream and specialist academic journals.

Furthermore, parapsychologists typically have little interest
in UFOs, astrology, occult beings, Bigfoot, or the Loch Ness
Monster. Their principal interest is in the capabilities and experiences of living human beings – hence the 'psychology' part of the
discipline's name. But 'para' means 'beyond', which signifies that
parapsychologists are particularly interested in exceptional or anomalous human capabilities and experiences. So, they are interested
in seemingly paranormal phenomena such as telepathy, clairvoyance, precognition, psychokinesis, out-of-body experiences, reincarnation, apparitions, hauntings, and spirit communication. The
University of Edinburgh's Koestler Parapsychology Unit (KPU), of
which I am a founder member, has studied many of these phenomena since its inception in 1985. Over these three decades, many
members of the public have contacted us to report their unusual
experiences. Throughout this book, I will delve into the KPU
archives to illustrate some of these experiences (to protect privacy,
some details have been changed and pseudonyms are used).

Finally, being a parapsychologist does not necessarily mean
that one believes in the existence of such phenomena. Although
many researchers find the evidence for psychic abilities convincing, others are less certain and some are even very sceptical. I
tend to take the middle position. I consider that there is sufficient
evidence to justify further work, but not enough to conclude that
paranormal abilities exist. Throughout this book, I will refer to

paranormal phenomena and abilities. For fluency of expression, I will avoid repeatedly using terms such as 'alleged', 'purported', and 'claimed', although this is not meant to imply that I think such phenomena are genuine.

It's now time to go back to the roots of parapsychology. The story begins with an age-old question: is there life after death?

The Fox sisters

For centuries paranormal phenomena were discussed and debated, but rarely subjected to systematic investigation. Then, in the mid-nineteenth century, two young girls set in motion a series of events that eventually led to the birth of modern-day parapsychology.

In March 1847, teenage sisters Kate and Margaret Fox from Hydesville in New York claimed to be able to talk to the dead. These strange conversations involved the sisters asking simple questions out loud and the 'spirits' apparently replying with a series of raps. The popularity of the sisters' demonstrations encouraged others to claim that they could also communicate with the dead. Early demonstrations often involved what became known as 'physical mediumship', wherein the spirits would make their presence known by rapping, moving objects, writing on slates, and even materializing limbs and figures. Over time other demonstrations involved so-called 'mental mediumship', wherein people would appear to enter a trance in order to channel messages from the dead, either directly from the deceased or with the supposed help of a spirit control.

Within a few years, hundreds of thousands of people became convinced that these demonstrations provided compelling evidence of life after death.

Although the majority of Victorian scientists were fiercely sceptical about the existence of paranormal phenomena, some researchers adopted a more open-minded approach towards the topic. Often driven by either a discomfort with the materialistic worldview or by personal bereavement, some of these academics invested considerable amounts of time and energy carrying out lengthy and intricate investigations.

A medium under the microscope

Several well-known Victorian scientists examined the existence of psychic ability, with one of the most important and influential studies being Sir William Crookes's investigation of Daniel Dunglas Home (pronounced 'Hume'). Crookes was a British chemist, a Fellow of the Royal Society, and a pioneer of the vacuum tube. In contrast, Home was a Scottish-born medium who claimed to be able to produce a range of psychic phenomena, including the ability to move heavy objects with the power of his mind and handle hot coals without burning himself.

In the early 1870s, Crookes carried out a series of studies into Home's claims, and eventually declared that Home could indeed demonstrate paranormal phenomena under controlled conditions. When Crookes published the results of this work in a well-respected scientific journal, many of his colleagues turned against him and argued that his investigations were deeply flawed. This criticism proved damaging to Crookes's career, with some academics even suggesting that his Fellowship of the Royal Society be revoked. Subsequently, Crookes became more cautious about publicizing his work with mediums, and only returned to openly publishing on the topic once he felt his position within academia was secure.

Worried that such career-damaging episodes would deter academics from investigating spirit communication, Spiritualist and writer Edmund Rogers proposed forming an organization that would place the scientific investigation of mediums on a more respectable footing. Rogers contacted several academics who were known to be positively predisposed to the paranormal, and suggested that they create a formal society. Rogers's work eventually led to the formation of the Society for Psychical Research in 1882.

Exact and unimpassioned enquiry

The Society for Psychical Research (SPR) was the world's first organization devoted to the scientific study of paranormal phenomena. Created by Rogers and a small group of highly eminent scholars, the SPR aimed to investigate 'that large body of debatable phenomena designated by such terms as mesmeric, psychical and "spiritualistic" ... in the same spirit of exact and unimpassioned enquiry which has enabled Science to solve so many problems'.

The SPR's first president was a respected moral philosopher from Cambridge University, Henry Sidgwick. Sidgwick's co-founders included classicist and poet Frederic Myers, psychologist Edmund Gurney, and mathematician (and Sidgwick's wife) Eleanor. Eleanor Sidgwick had been born into arguably the most influential political dynasty in nineteenth-century Britain, and her brothers – politician Gerald Balfour and future British Prime Minister Arthur Balfour – also played key roles in forming the Society. This inner circle of scholars and politicians was soon joined by an illustrious group of scientists, including Sir William Crookes, physicist Sir William Barrett, Nobel laureate physicist Sir Joseph John Thomson, and physicist Sir Oliver Lodge.

Many of the SPR's founding fathers were drawn to the organization out of intellectual curiosity, while others were eager to have science confirm their religious beliefs. Sir Oliver Lodge, for instance, was a committed Christian who believed that the human spirit survived physical death, and William Barrett was a strong Spiritualist. However, despite their differing motivations and beliefs, all of the founders were prepared to align themselves with the SPR's stated goal, namely to examine: 'without prejudice or prepossession and in a scientific spirit those faculties of man, real or supposed, which appear to be inexplicable on any generally recognized hypothesis'.

Membership of the SPR soon swelled, and its researchers started to work with scientists on the European Continent, including French physiologist and future Nobel Prize-winner Charles Richet. In 1885, Harvard philosopher William James helped psychical researchers on either side of the Atlantic to collaborate by forming the American Society for Psychical Research (ASPR).

Initial work

Much of the early SPR research focused on one of the three strands of work central to modern-day parapsychology, namely testing those claiming strong mediumistic and psychic powers. Unfortunately for those wanting to believe in evidence of an afterlife, many of those producing demonstrations of physical mediumship were caught dressing up and impersonating spirits, employing accomplices, and using magic tricks to create séance phenomena. As a result, many SPR researchers started to turn their attention away from spirit raps and manifestations, and towards demonstrations of mental mediumship. This work entailed psychical researchers documenting the messages that allegedly came from the dead and then trying to ascertain the accuracy of those messages. The investigations proved time-consuming and controversial, with sceptics arguing, for example, that the mediums may have discovered the information through normal means, or that the messages were vague and therefore open to interpretation.

Lengthy reports describing investigations into physical and mental mediumship were published in the SPR's *Journal* and *Proceedings*. Proponents of the paranormal believed that this large body of work proved the existence of mediumistic and psychic powers, while sceptics argued that the research had only yielded evidence of self-deception and trickery.

THE CREERY SISTERS

Whereas mediums claim to be able to communicate with the dead, psychics claim that they possess the ability to read minds, see into the future, or reveal concealed information. Some SPR research involved examining those claiming psychic powers. In 1882, for example, the respected physicist Sir William Barrett investigated the telepathic abilities of the Creery family from Derbyshire in the UK. The Reverend A.M. Creery ('a clergyman of unblemished character') had contacted the SPR and described a series of informal experiments that he had conducted with his daughters. During these experiments, Creery's daughters appeared able to read his mind, and the Reverend invited the SPR to stage a more formal investigation. Intrigued, the SPR researchers travelled to the Creerys' house and carried out a series of studies with the family over a six-year period. During Barrett's experiments, one of Creery's daughters would first leave the room. Those remaining in the room would then randomly select an object, or playing card, and the absent daughter would then return to the room and attempt to psychically identify the object or card. The researchers reported that the girls were often accurate, and concluded that the sisters did indeed possess some form of telepathic ability. However, in a later series of studies, Henry and Eleanor Sidgwick caught two of the children secretly exchanging information about the target via subtle movements of their head and feet.

These sorts of investigations highlight a key aspect of research into strong psychic claims, namely that those carrying out such work need to understand the psychology of deception.

Philosopher and psychologist John Beloff has referred to the early years of the SPR as the 'heroic age' of psychical research, with the founders expanding their horizons and examining paranormal phenomena beyond spirit communication. In fact, within a year of the SPR's foundation, researchers started to explore a second strand of enquiry that is central to modern-day parapsychology, namely the investigation of anomalous experiences.

This work took several different forms. For example, in 1886, psychologist Edmund Gurney carried out a painstaking analysis of over seven hundred reports of people claiming to have seen an apparition of someone who, at that very moment, was either dying or in a life-threatening situation. Similarly, Henry and Eleanor Sidgwick conducted a 'Census of Hallucinations', asking over seventeen thousand people whether they had experienced an apparition. Once again, this work generated a great deal of controversy, with some believing that the mass of seemingly reliable accounts proved the existence of apparitions, while others argued that witnesses may have embellished their experience or may have been hallucinating.

The birth of laboratory-based investigations

The year 1884 saw the birth of the third strand of parapsychological research, namely laboratory-based investigations into psychic ability. Unlike the tests into individuals claiming strong abilities, this work tends to focus on the notion that most people have some form of weak, latent ability. As a result, the work generally involves testing large numbers of people (who don't necessarily claim to be psychic) and pooling the results. This type of research tends to use statistics to assess the outcome of tests. Some of the earliest work of this kind was conducted by French researcher Charles Richet. Richet carried out a series of clairvoyance experiments in which a hypnotized volunteer was asked to try to psychically determine the identity of hidden playing cards. Richet reported the results from over a hundred trials and claimed that they supported the evidence of psychic ability.

Stanford psychologist John Edgar Coover published the results of the first university-based ESP experiments in America in 1917. Reporting findings from four large studies, and over ten thousand trials, Coover noted that he had found no evidence of ESP (a conclusion disputed by Richet). Although Coover reported null results, his work demonstrated that it was possible to carry out parapsychology research within an academic setting.

In 1927, psychologist William McDougall moved from Harvard to head the Psychology Department at Duke University. McDougall's positive attitude towards the possible existence of paranormal phenomena resulted in his inviting plant physiologist Joseph Banks (J.B.) Rhine to set up America's first parapsychology laboratory at Duke. Rhine accepted the offer and remained in position until his retirement in 1966.

Distancing himself from research into the possible existence of life after death, Rhine laid the foundations for modern-day laboratory research into psychic ability. Rhine helped develop a special deck of twenty-five cards for ESP testing, with each of the cards containing one of five geometrical symbols (a circle, cross, wavy lines, square, or cross). In a typical experiment, researchers would shuffle the deck of cards and then ask volunteers to try to guess the order of the deck. Twenty per cent of the volunteer's guesses should be correct by chance alone, with any above-chance scoring being seen as evidence for psychic ability. Later work involved investigating the existence of psychokinesis by asking volunteers to mentally influence the roll of dice.

Rhine argued that the results of his studies supported the existence of psychic ability. In contrast, sceptics attributed the results to various methodological and statistical shortcomings. Whatever the truth about his findings, there is little disagreement about the contribution Rhine made towards establishing parapsychology as an academic discipline. In 1937, for example, Rhine established the *Journal of Parapsychology*. This peer-reviewed journal still exists, and provides one of the main outlets for parapsychologists to disseminate their work to the academic community. In 1957, Rhine helped to found parapsychology's professional body, the Parapsychological Association (PA). In 1969, the PA was accepted as an affiliate member of the American Association for the Advancement of Science, and is currently made up of about three hundred members worldwide.

Rhine's sponsor, McDougall, described how in the mid-1960s the 'smouldering resentment' of Rhine's colleagues in the Department of Psychology meant that his laboratory was no longer welcome at Duke University. Eventually, Rhine set up a new independent research institute, The Foundation for Research into the Nature of Man, close to the Duke campus. This institute still survives today, and has recently been renamed as the Rhine Research Center.

THE SCEPTICS

Investigations into psychic phenomena are both controversial and complex, and scepticism has always played an important role in such work. Much of the best-informed and most productive criticism has come from those working within parapsychology. However, sceptics from outside the field have also played a key role. Some of these sceptics have formed organizations to help carry out and promote this work, with perhaps the best known of these being the Committee for Scientific Investigation of Claims of the Paranormal (or CSICOP).

In the early 1970s, humanist philosopher Paul Kurtz noticed a surge of public interest in the paranormal, and decided to establish an organization devoted to the critical examination of seemingly paranormal phenomena. Kurtz joined forces with several like-minded colleagues, including science writer Martin Gardner, psychologist Ray Hyman, and magician James Randi, and formed CSICOP. Randi's activities have sometimes been criticized (we will encounter his famous 'Project Alpha' later). However, parapsychology's research methods have also benefited from the work of a few well-informed sceptics.

Over the years, CSICOP has helped promote scepticism on a wide variety of topics, including investigations into psychics, work examining the psychology of deception and self-deception, and critiques of laboratory-based parapsychology experiments. Much of this work has been reported at CSICOP conferences and published in their bi-monthly magazine, *Skeptical Inquirer*.

In 2006, the organization shortened its name to the Committee for Skeptical Inquiry (CSI), and most recently it has broadened its remit, presenting a sceptical view on a wide range of topics including creationism, conspiracy theories, and climate change denial. The fact that less attention is now devoted to experimental parapsychology may be an indication that, in general, sceptics no longer see it as an easy target.

Modern-day parapsychology

Rhine's pioneering work paved the way for several other American parapsychological laboratories throughout the 1960s and 1970s. For example, in 1966, the Maimonides Dream Laboratory in New York carried out ground-breaking research into dream telepathy and precognition; in 1974, the Stanford Research Institute examined the possible existence of remote viewing; and, in 1979, the Princeton Engineering Anomalies Research Laboratory began a series of studies into the possible existence of psychokinesis. During the 1980s, parapsychology continued to flourish, with academics across Europe carrying out research into the topic, including work in Britain studying anomalous experiences (University of Bristol); research in the Netherlands investigating precognition and physical theories of psi (Universities of Utrecht and Amsterdam); work in France studying micro–PK (L'Institut Métapsychique Internationale in Paris); ESP research in Sweden (University of Gothenburg); and in Germany the study of remote mental influence over living systems (Institut für Grenzgebiete der Psychologie und Psychohygiene, in Freiburg). In 1985, the University of Edinburgh established the Koestler Chair in Parapsychology (see box).

ROBERT MORRIS AND THE KOESTLER PARAPSYCHOLOGY UNIT

In the mid-1970s, the noted writer Arthur Koestler was diagnosed with Parkinson's disease, and in 1980 with chronic lymphocytic leukaemia. In 1983, Koestler and his wife Cynthia felt unable to face the continued physical decline associated with the illnesses, and committed a joint suicide. Koestler had a lifelong interest in the paranormal and bequeathed almost his entire estate to establish a Chair of Parapsychology at a British university. Philosopher John Beloff from the University of Edinburgh had devoted much of his career to parapsychology, and played a key role in persuading his university to accept Koestler's bequest. In 1985, Robert Morris was appointed Koestler Professor of Parapsychology, and held the position until his death in 2004. Morris had previously worked with Rhine at Duke University, and had lectured on parapsychology at the University of California, Santa Barbara.

Morris was instrumental in the formation and growth of the Koestler Parapsychology Unit, recruiting additional staff, overseeing over a hundred undergraduate projects, and supervising more than thirty postgraduate students. Many of these postgraduate students went on to research and teach parapsychology at other universities. Morris was also passionate about integrating parapsychology into the wider academic community, serving as president of the Psychology section of the British Science Association.

I worked with Morris throughout his time at Edinburgh and, following his untimely death, was appointed to one of two newly formed lectureships that are supported by the Koestler bequest.

Unfortunately, parapsychological research in America has declined considerably since the 1980s, with many laboratories (including the Maimonides Medical Center Dream Laboratory, the Psychophysical Research Laboratories, and the Princeton Engineering Anomalies Research Laboratory) no longer operating often because of a lack of funding. As a result, most American research into parapsychology now takes place at privately funded institutions, such as the Institute of Noetic Sciences in California. The Division of Perceptual Studies at the University of Virginia is an exception to this picture, and a few US parapsychologists such as Rex Stanford and Stanley Krippner also hold positions at universities. However, in the UK and Europe, parapsychology seems to have a firmer foothold in academia. Work continues at several British universities (including the University of Edinburgh and Goldsmiths, University of London), and several new sources of funding for parapsychology have opened up in Europe, including the endowment of a professorship to study consciousness and anomalous experiences at the University of Lund in Sweden. In addition, after completing their studies at the Koestler Parapsychology Unit, many postgraduate students obtained lectureships where they introduced parapsychology teaching and research to several British universities, including the Universities of Hertfordshire, Northampton, and Greenwich.

This book presents an overview of the three main strands of work involved in parapsychology. **Section 1** focuses on testing those claiming strong psychic abilities. This work dates back to the turn of the last century, and involves examining those claiming psychokinesis (including metal bending, materialization, and telekinesis); ESP in the real world (including psychic readings, remote viewing, and psychic detection); and mediums who appear able to receive messages from the dead. **Section 2** focuses on anomalous experiences, including the psychological mechanisms that might underlie psychic experiences in everyday life, instances of ghostly sightings and haunted locations, and research into out-of-body experiences and near-death experiences. **Section 3** focuses on laboratory-based studies into the possible existence of psychic ability, including work into telepathy and clairvoyance, precognition, and psychokinesis.

All three sections reflect the controversial nature of the field, presenting an overview of the evidence that seems to support the existence of the paranormal, and the criticisms that have been levelled at this work.

Section 1
Testing psychic claimants

2
Macro-PK

From the archive ...

A few years ago, my friends and I watched a video of a guy who said he could bend metal by the power of his mind. We didn't really believe what we saw on the film, but later on, just for a laugh, we started fooling around with some of my mum's cutlery. It's hard to describe what happened next. I was just lightly holding the handle of a spoon, and my friend was stroking the metal between the handle and the bowl. Suddenly my pal shouted that the metal was becoming hot, and I could see the bowl of the spoon starting to droop. The metal between the handle and the bowl seemed to get flexible. I swear I didn't have to force it at all, it bent quite easily, right back so the bowl was pointing in the opposite direction to normal. I still can't quite explain what happened. My mum wasn't pleased that we'd spoiled her cutlery, but I've still got the bent spoon. How do you explain that?

(Kevin, aged 20)

Large-scale psychokinesis (or, as it is usually referred to, 'macro-PK') is the ability to psychically influence objects. Individuals claiming to possess this ability exhibit a wide variety of phenomena, including, for example, metal bending, levitation, and materializations. In the 1970s, for instance, Uri Geller caused a sensation by claiming to be able to bend metal such as spoons psychically. There was even an outbreak of 'mini-Gellerism', as children began to demonstrate the same effects. Had Geller somehow awakened their latent psychokinetic abilities? Innocent children wouldn't be faking it, would they? Perhaps not surprisingly, investigations into such claims have generated a considerable amount of debate and controversy.

The 'thoughtography' controversy

In the early 1960s, a Chicago elevator operator named Ted Serios claimed that he could paranormally cause images to appear on photographic film. First, Serios would hold a small black tube to his forehead (which he said helped to focus his thought waves), then he would place the tube in front of the lens of a Polaroid camera and trigger the camera. Most of the resulting photographs were just blank prints, but some showed indistinct shapes or slightly blurry images of buildings and geographical locations.

Intrigued by Serios's claims, University of Colorado psychiatrist Jule Eisenbud conducted tests with Serios in a private hospital in the city. Eisenbud quickly discovered that the work was going to be challenging, in part, because Serios tended to resist authority and frequently created disruption around himself. He would often become aggressively drunk and abusive, running around the room half-naked, and making ridiculous demands on those present. With sessions often lasting four or five hours, Eisenbud struggled to continually observe and record what was happening. Nevertheless, eventually Eisenbud became convinced that Serios did indeed possess genuine paranormal powers. Eisenbud presented a detailed account of his investigations in the 1967 book *The World of Ted Serios: 'Thoughtographic' Studies of an Extraordinary Mind*.

Eisenbud's book was positively received by the public but ridiculed by many academics. (Writing in *The New York Times*, psychologist Hans Eysenck noted, 'Dr. Eisenbud seems to have little notion of what experiments are and less liking for the rigors and methodological niceties of scientific research.')

Eventually, other researchers decided to conduct their own enquiries. An administrator at the hospital where Eisenbud had conducted some of his investigations with Serios became concerned at this use of hospital facilities. He sponsored the hospital's communications director, a photographer named Nile Root, to investigate. Root subsequently described how his suspicions were aroused when Eisenbud showed him one of Serios's 'thoughtographs':

> One image displayed dots, the same as those seen in a news-paper reproduction. The dots were magnified, sharp in the center of the image and blurred at the edges. This indicated to me that this image was a copy of a newspaper halftone engrav-ing made with an uncorrected closeup lens.

Root then observed Serios in action. Towards the end of a five-hour session with an increasingly intoxicated Serios, Root claims to have spotted a shiny object inside the tube that Serios was holding in front of the camera. Root subsequently found he could generate similar 'thoughtographs' by using short focal-length lenses and small transparencies.

The respected science magazine *Scientific American* also arranged for a small team of expert photographers and magi-cians (including skilled magician and Harvard statistician Persi Diaconis) to conduct their own investigation into Serios. The team travelled to Denver and watched Serios attempt to demon-strate his abilities for a television crew. Diaconis was less than impressed with the measures in place to prevent possible cheat-ing. For example, the crew had brought their own Polaroid film, however Diaconis was able to switch some of their samples with his own packets of film. Diaconis also described how he thought he saw Serios covertly load something into the tube, but was not permitted to inspect the device. Subsequently, Diaconis and his photographer colleagues discovered several ways in which they could duplicate Serios's photographic effects, for instance by inserting a small image into the tube.

Eisenbud and his colleague Professor Stephen Braude from the University of Maryland Baltimore County responded to these criticisms by pointing out that sceptics have been unable to replicate Serios's effects under similar experimental controls, and that sleight-of-hand was ruled out in later tests where Serios had no physical contact with the camera at the time the picture was taken. However, many sceptics believe that Eisenbud's lack of conjuring knowledge, combined with Serios's unruly and disruptive behaviour, rendered these later experiments far from fraud-proof. Mathematician and sceptic Martin Gardner later concluded, 'The parapsychologists who once took Ted Serios and others like him seriously would have been spared their embarrassments had they known anything about magic.'

Braude went on to write a book about his adventures testing psychic claimants, revealing just how difficult it is to conduct well-controlled tests even when using modern technology to record events (see box).

THE GOLD LEAF LADY

The story of 'Katie, the Gold Leaf Lady' is noteworthy because this unusual case of paranormal materialization was still active when parapsychologist and philosopher Professor Stephen Braude reported it in 1997. So the events occurred at a time when researchers had easy access to inexpensive but good-quality video technology.

Braude describes Katie as a 'functionally illiterate' Florida housewife in her mid-fifties. Katie claimed that a delicate gold-coloured foil would spontaneously appear on her skin (chemical analysis revealed the foil was brass). Several witnesses reportedly saw this happen to her.

Attempts to document the spontaneous emergence of the foil during Katie's everyday life, by following her with video cameras, were unsuccessful. Researchers also conducted more systematic investigations, which involved Katie being thoroughly searched by her physician (including removal of her dentures) and then seated in front of one or more video cameras while she chatted with observers. During these sessions, the foil would typically appear on Katie's abdomen, but behind her shirt so that the foil's appearance was never caught on camera. Braude only once managed to film foil seemingly emerging. This happened on Katie's face, after she rubbed her eye a few times with her finger, but her hand went out of camera shot during the episode.

Los Angeles magician Christopher Chacon was brought in to advise on Katie's case. He confirmed that the foil was extremely difficult to handle and reportedly concluded that she could not have inconspicuously placed it on her body while observed. The mystery of Katie remains unsolved. The claimed phenomena were never unambiguously captured on film, and the Gold Leaf Lady case illustrates how difficult it is, even with the benefit of modern technology, to investigate claims of paranormal physical phenomena.

Mind-bending metal bending

In the 1970s, Uri Geller gained worldwide notoriety by claiming to be able to deform metal psychokinetically. Geller was born in Tel Aviv in 1946, and as a young man performed magic shows in theatres throughout Israel. Geller impressed his audiences with a range of demonstrations including identifying concealed pictures, bending metal objects, and making stopped watches restart.

News quickly spread of Geller's seemingly remarkable abilities, and in November 1973 he was invited to appear on the BBC television programme *The Dimbleby Talk-In*. Geller and host David Dimbleby were joined by John Taylor, a professor of applied mathematics at King's College London. During the programme, Geller selected a fork from a tray of objects, and had Dimbleby lightly hold one end while Geller gently stroked the other end. The fork appeared to bend and break. A few minutes later Geller pointed out that another fork on the table appeared to be bending of its own accord. Within hours of the broadcast, the BBC began receiving calls from members of the public claiming that cutlery in their own homes had bent, and stopped watches had restarted.

John Taylor was baffled by what he had witnessed during the programme and wondered if Geller could replicate the demonstration under more controlled conditions. In February 1974, Geller agreed to be tested at Taylor's laboratory. The university's metallurgical department prepared aluminium and copper samples, some of which were sealed in glass or wire mesh tubes. Two of Taylor's colleagues observed while Geller attempted to exert his psychokinetic powers on the samples. Taylor reported that some of the samples did indeed bend, although the observers had not seen the deformation occur. Shaken by these results, Taylor summarized his conclusions in his 1975 book *Superminds*:

> The Geller effect – of metal-bending – is clearly not brought about by fraud. It is so exceptional it presents a crucial challenge to modern science and could even destroy the latter if no explanation became available.

Taylor's conclusion proved premature. He tested several other people claiming to possess the same type of metal-bending psychokinetic ability, but discovered no evidence of paranormal forces at work. Taylor's position was weakened even further when magician and sceptic James Randi visited his office incognito and found that he could easily circumvent Taylor's experimental controls.

This was not the only time Randi helped play an important role in undermining Geller's claims. When Geller demonstrated his feats on talk shows, Randi would later appear on the show and replicate Geller's stunts using simple conjuring techniques (often noting, 'If Uri Geller bends spoons with divine powers, then he's doing it the hard way'). Randi showed that there are numerous ways in which spoon bending can be faked. One of the most effective methods is to pre-weaken the metal by repeatedly bending it back and forth until it is about to fracture. The prepared spoon can then be placed in the pile of cutlery and is subsequently selected by the 'psychic' when the time comes to demonstrate their skills. At this point, even a gentle touch will cause the spoon to bend and then break. Another commonly employed technique is to momentarily direct the audience's attention elsewhere, enabling the 'psychic' to use sleight-of-hand to bend the metal. The 'psychic' conceals the bend and then gradually reveals it after the audience's gaze returns to the spoon.

Other sceptics attempted to account for the reports of bent cutlery in people's homes. For example, New Zealand psychologists David Marks and Richard Kammann pointed out that almost anyone who searches carefully will find a bent fork or spoon in their house. In addition, Marks and Kammann visited seven jewellery stores and obtained over one hundred broken watches. Fifty-seven per cent of the watches started ticking again when warmed by being held in a person's hand for a few minutes.

The scientific community grew increasingly sceptical about psychokinetic metal-bending claims (see box) and eventually Taylor recanted his initial endorsement, noting: 'We have searched for the supernatural and not found it. In the main, only poor experimentation, shoddy theory, and human gullibility have been encountered.'

MINI-GELLERS

In November 1973, Uri Geller demonstrated his apparent metal-bending skills on the popular British children's television show *Blue Peter*. His performance was watched by millions of viewers and resulted in some children suddenly claiming that they too could bend metal using just the power of their mind. Eventually, Professor John Taylor (who had previously tested Geller at his laboratory) decided to investigate several of these so-called 'mini-Gellers', but quickly discovered that they could only produce their feats when unobserved.

In the early 1970s, sociologist Harry Collins and physicist Brian Pamplin (both from the University of Bath) decided to discover whether they could catch the children cheating. The researchers invited six mini-Gellers to their laboratory and then secretly filmed through a two-way mirror as the children attempted to demonstrate their abilities in the presence of laboratory staff. Pamplin and Collins had instructed the staff periodically to relax their vigilance. Reporting their findings in the highly prestigious scientific journal *Nature*, Pamplin and Collins described how their film revealed evidence of the mini-Gellers taking advantage of these moments of apparent laxity, and furtively using force to bend the objects.

The deceptiveness of the children shouldn't be underestimated. In 1975, magician David Berglas set up a metal-bending competition and arranged for several 'mini-Gellers' to be carefully observed by those well versed in conjuring. In line with the findings of Pamplin and Collins, the youngsters were seen using physical force to bend the cutlery when they thought they were unobserved, with the observers noting that 'the subtlety, perceptiveness and gall of children as young as seven came as a rude shock'.

Distant influence: God moves in mysterious ways

Around the same time as Uri Geller was making his name bending spoons, a martial-arts expert called James Hydrick stunned American television audiences with his telekinetic abilities.

Hydrick had experienced a troubled childhood. Born in South Carolina in 1959, he was abandoned by an alcoholic mother when he was only three years old, and was left in the care of his father. Following suggestions that the boy was suffering physical abuse, social services took him into care. Behavioural problems led to Hydrick being moved from one foster family to another until, aged eighteen, he ended up in the Los Angeles County jail following a conviction for kidnapping and robbery. While in jail, Hydrick became fascinated with martial arts, and trained intensively to develop impressive feats of strength, speed, and agility. Hydrick also started to develop his repertoire of apparently miraculous powers, including the ability to move objects with his mind. Hydrick used his apparent gifts to the full, often manipulating his fellow inmates, and even his captors, by seemingly invoking God to turn the pages of the prison Bible – without Hydrick touching them.

On release from prison, Hydrick opened a martial-arts gym in Salt Lake City, Utah. He began wearing an eastern costume, called himself 'Song Chai', and claimed that he had learned from a Chinese master how to use mental powers to influence physical objects. To convince doubters, Hydrick would demonstrate his supposed paranormal abilities by, for instance, apparently causing the gym's roof to creak and heavy punchbags to swing back and forth without anyone touching them. Having thereby acquired guru-like status in his local area, Hydrick soon attracted the attention of the national media.

In December 1980, Hydrick appeared on ABC's popular programme *That's Incredible*. He began with his mysterious mental page-turning demonstration, then balanced a pencil horizontally over the edge of a table and appeared to use the power of his mind to make the pencil pivot back and forth. The audience was stunned by Hydrick's apparent telekinetic abilities and he quickly rose to national fame.

Magician and sceptic James Randi suspected that Hydrick moved objects simply by blowing puffs of air towards them.

Randi explained how, to an inexpert eye, Hydrick's trick was deceptive because he emitted the air surreptitiously through only slightly parted lips and then turned his head so he was facing away from the objects by the time they moved. Randi offered Hydrick $10,000 if he could convince a panel of expert scientists that his abilities were paranormal.

Perhaps surprisingly, Hydrick accepted Randi's challenge, and the event was recorded by the popular TV show *That's My Line* in February 1981. For the page-turning test, Randi placed an open telephone directory on a table and then ingeniously scattered styrofoam particles around it. Any air blown towards the directory would immediately become evident from the movement of the particles. For over an hour, Hydrick failed to use his supposed mental powers to move the pages of the book. The judges unanimously agreed that Hydrick had shown no paranormal abilities, but Hydrick maintained that his powers had simply deserted him on that occasion. Despite this humiliating episode, a few months later, Hydrick accepted another invitation to demonstrate his skills in front of the camera, this time from an undercover magician called Danny Korem.

Korem was a skilled magician and evangelical Christian who both debunked 'miracle-mongers' but praised the 'genuine magic' of Jesus. Korem secretly mastered Hydrick's air-blowing technique and then asked the psychic if he would like to feature in a documentary. After filming Hydrick performing his usual array of feats, Korem asked him if he would transfer some of his paranormal abilities to Korem. Hydrick agreed and meditated as he held his hands over Korem's. Then, employing the air-puffing technique that he had previously perfected, Korem moved a pencil in front of a visibly shocked Hydrick.

The game was finally up, and Hydrick agreed to give a filmed confession to Korem in which he revealed all of the tricks of his trade. For example, Hydrick explained that his psychokinetic movement of the heavy punchbags at his gym was simply due to solar energy. Around the same time every day, the sun's heat caused the roof to expand and the punchbags to sway. All Hydrick had to do was gather his students at the right time, and suggest to them that he was causing the phenomena.

In 1989, Hydrick was sentenced to seventeen years in jail after molesting five boys whom he'd attracted with his supposed psychic stunts. He is now residing in a maximum security facility.

NINA KULAGINA

Born in Leningrad in 1926, Nina Kulagina is perhaps one of the best-known Soviet psychic stars. Kulagina claimed that, as a child, objects in her vicinity moved when she was angry. During the Cold War, film emerged of Kulagina gesturing over small objects on a table, and seemingly causing them to move across the table. She was also filmed apparently deflecting the needle of a compass that was shielded under a transparent dome.

A small number of Western scientists were permitted to study Kulagina, including Joseph Gaither Pratt from the University of Virginia. After carefully watching her demonstrations, Pratt concluded that her feats were 'suggestive of PK ability'. Many of her seemingly paranormal accomplishments were filmed but Kulagina was never caught cheating. However, various researchers have attempted to explain her feats. In 1978, physicist John Taylor from King's College London measured electrostatic charges while psychic claimants attempted without touching to deflect compass needles and move straws that were shielded by glass and perspex domes. The objects clearly moved without any visible contact, but Taylor discovered that this was due to a build-up of electrostatic charges. When earthing was used to prevent these charges accumulating, the movements ceased. This electrostatic explanation, however, would not account for those instances when Kulagina was said to have moved objects from several feet away. Undeterred, sceptics have pointed out that the test conditions may have permitted trickery, and that the Soviets, as part of the Cold War, were keen to convince the West that they had uncovered individuals with genuine psychic ability.

'Miracles are my visiting cards'

Several Eastern religious leaders claim to be able to materialize small precious objects for their followers. It is often difficult to research these claims as many of these individuals are unwilling to take part in controlled investigations. However, Icelandic parapsychologist Professor Erlendur Haraldsson has studied perhaps the best known of these claimants, a charismatic Indian guru dubbed the 'Uri Geller of the East'.

Sai Baba was born in 1926 in a remote village in Northern India. Around the age of thirteen, he announced that he was the reincarnation of a spiritual leader, and convinced others by materializing sweets, flowers, and food. His following quickly grew, with Sai Baba frequently dispensing spiritual guidance to his devotees. During meetings, Sai Baba would often make a strange circular gesture with his palm facing downwards and produce a powdery stream of 'vibhuti' (a sacred ash), as well as gold and silver jewellery. Sai Baba did this with such ease that he would claim that these so-called 'miracles' were merely his visiting cards.

In the mid-1970s, Erlendur Haraldsson and his colleague Karlis Osis investigated Sai Baba's paranormal materializations. During several visits, the researchers observed Sai Baba produce many objects, but none under controlled conditions. However, they were especially impressed by one incident involving a large gold ring that Sai Baba had gifted to Osis on their first visit. The ring had contained an enamelled portrait of Sai Baba, but, during one of their later interviews, Sai Baba pointed out that the portrait was missing from the ring. Two days after that, Sai Baba took the empty ring from Osis then asked him whether he would like the same or a different picture back. Osis replied that he would like the same picture. Sai Baba seemed to make the old ring disappear, then opened his fist to reveal a slightly different ring containing what appeared to be the original portrait.

In 1992, Sai Baba's reputation became tarnished after he appeared to be caught faking a materialization during the opening of a hall that had been built in his honour. A film from the event shows Sai Baba on stage and about to present a trophy that will be brought to him by an assistant. As the assistant passes the trophy to Sai Baba, their hands meet and fumble for a few moments below the object, as if he is secretly receiving an object from his assistant. Having presented the award, Sai Baba then proceeds to make his usual circular materialization gestures and 'produces' a gold chain. A few years later, numerous other allegations of fraud, sexual abuse, and violence by Sai Baba emerged.

Magicians who have studied Sai Baba's productions argue that they bear the hallmarks of techniques used by conjurors. Sai Baba was always in control of what was produced, and when. Regarding the ring incident reported by Haraldsson and Osis, it was Sai Baba who pointed out that the portrait was missing, then he had two days in which to obtain two possible substitute rings. He then chose the moment to switch the broken ring by employing misdirection and sleight-of-hand. The incident at the presentation ceremony also indicates that, as many magicians do, he employed accomplices to help him produce his seemingly miraculous feats.

Sai Baba never consented to be tested under conditions that would preclude sleight-of-hand. However, another Indian guru who produced similar 'miraculous' materializations did agree to such an investigation. In the early 1990s, Haraldsson teamed up with magician and parapsychologist Professor Richard Wiseman, and the two of them travelled to India to investigate a guru named Swami Premananda. Like Sai Baba, Premananda had a large following and appeared to be able to produce objects in his left hand at will. To test this claim, the investigators first washed and inspected Premananda's left hand and encased it in a clear plastic bag that was then sealed at his wrist. This prevented the guru from secretly transferring any objects to his hand prior to producing them within the bag.

Premananda was never able to produce any trinkets or vibhuti while the controls were in place. He *was* able to do so once the bag was removed, but crucially only following a well-timed movement of his left hand to the folds of his robes in his lap. This move was made while Premananda attempted to divert the researchers' attention by declaring the test over, smiling and engaging them in eye contact. Haraldsson and Wiseman concluded that their filmed evidence was consistent with Premananda faking the materializations by covertly retrieving objects from his robes when people's attention was distracted.

'THE FIRST PSYCHIC'

Peter Lamont, of the University of Edinburgh's Koestler Parapsychology Unit, has described the medium D.D. Home as 'the first psychic'. Home's remarkable physical feats attracted the attention of eminent scientists such as William Crookes, as well as the 'high society' of the English literary scene, and tsars, emperors, and royalty across the European Continent. Home's best-known feat occurred in December 1868, in Ashley House, London. He was said to have levitated horizontally out of one open third-floor window and in through another, as described by the future Earl of Crawford, Lord Adare, and his cousin Captain Charles Wynne.

Home had a reputation as an honest medium. His séances took place in dim light rather than complete darkness, and a wide range of physical phenomena were attested to by numerous apparently reliable witnesses. Home disarmingly made himself available free of charge both to researchers and the curious public. Sceptical psychical researcher Frank Podmore stated of Home that 'there is no evidence of any weight that he was even privately detected in trickery', unlike most other nineteenth-century mediums. Despite considerable incredulity at Crookes's investigations, sceptical scientists never convincingly debunked Home's feats.

Towards a psychology of psychic fraud

Given the investigations outlined so far, it perhaps isn't surprising that most parapsychologists do not believe that there exists a strong body of evidence supporting the existence of macro-PK. However, investigations into such claims have yielded a considerable insight into the psychology used to fool observers into thinking that they have witnessed genuine psychic ability.

Time misdirection. People only begin to pay attention when a fake psychic appears to start to perform. With a demonstration of spoon bending, this might be the case when the fake psychic picks up the spoon and begins rubbing it. However, the actual trick may have started some time before when the fake psychic secretly and repeatedly bent the bowl of the spoon back and forth to pre-weaken it.

Verbal suggestion. Those claiming metal-bending abilities frequently place a bent key or spoon on the table and then exclaim, 'Look, it's still bending!' Witnesses agree that they can see the object continue to bend without any physical contact by the psychic. In 2005, psychologists Richard Wiseman and Emma Greening created two films in which a fake psychic placed a bent key on a table. The key never moved after it was put down and the films were identical except for the soundtrack. One group of participants heard the fake psychic state that the key was still bending, while the other group did not hear any verbal suggestion. Participants in the 'it's still bending' group were more likely to report seeing the key bend after it had been put down. Furthermore, those who had seen the key continue to bend tended to forget the fake psychic's verbal suggestion. The witness is thus likely to be persuaded of the psychic's 'abilities', because they have forgotten vital conflicting information.

Controlling attention. Ted Serios stretched the observational powers of investigators to their limits by staging sessions that lasted for several hours and creating a chaotic and distracting environment. In contrast, other performers make use of a phenomenon known as 'inattentional blindness'. This phenomenon was dramatically demonstrated in a 1999 study by Harvard University psychologist Dan Simons. Simons filmed two teams of basketball players, one of which wore white T-shirts, while the other team wore black. Each team moved around and passed a basketball between themselves, and Simons asked observers to count the number of passes made between the white team. During the film, a man dressed in a gorilla suit saunters through the players, turns and faces the camera, beats his chest, then exits stage left. Only 42% of observers spotted the gorilla, because their attention was focused on the basketball. In short, people often fail to see obvious and surprising events simply because they are not focusing on them. Fake psychics can use this phenomenon to their advantage. For example, during his 'page-turning' feat, James Hydrick would look away from the book at the precise moment at which he was subtly directing a puff of breath towards it. In doing so, Hydrick diverted attention away from his face, making it less likely that the audience would notice the puff of air.

Framing. People perceive a psychic demonstration through a 'frame' shaped by their beliefs and expectations. If the audience believes they are watching a conjuror, they will be vigilant for hidden mirrors, sleight-of-hand, and technical wizardry. If they believe they are watching someone with miraculous powers, they may not be looking out for trickery. This principle seems to play a key role during the paranormal materializations of small objects by religious leaders like Sai Baba. Devotees are convinced that the guru's productions of vibhuti and jewellery are miraculous signs of his elevated spiritual status. By viewing Sai Baba as a god-man, his followers seek confirmation of his holy powers, and are satisfied when they see evidence of these supposed powers.

Memory. Soon after witnessing a magic trick or demonstration of psychic ability, people try to remember what they have seen. Unfortunately, their beliefs and biases can affect their memory of the performance. In one study, psychologists Richard Wiseman and Robert Morris showed volunteers film footage of a fake psychic seemingly using macro-PK powers to bend a fork. In reality, the film clearly showed the performer switching an examined fork for one that had been prepared beforehand. Viewers were later asked what details they could remember from the film. Compared to those who believed in the paranormal, those subjects who were sceptical about the paranormal recalled more details relevant to how the metal bending was faked. Because the believers were more likely to accept that they were watching a genuine psychic, they attended less to aspects of the demonstration that would have indicated cheating, and therefore subsequently could not remember these vital moments.

Parapsychologist beware! Project Alpha

Investigations into macro-PK have contributed to our understanding of the psychology of deception and observation. However, they have also impacted on research practice within parapsychology. As we have seen, some researchers who attempted to investigate claims of macro-PK didn't possess the conjuring knowledge necessary for such research. In the late 1970s, magician and sceptic James Randi carried out a landmark and controversial hoax in order to highlight the need for such expertise when studying such claims.

The story begins with the aviation pioneer James McDonnell. As an undergraduate student at Princeton, James had considered a career in parapsychology but was persuaded to study engineering. However, McDonnell never lost his fascination with the paranormal, and in 1979 he donated $500,000 to the University of Washington to set up a parapsychology laboratory. Physicist Peter

Phillips took up the directorship of the McDonnell Laboratory for Psychical Research (colloquially known as 'MacLab') and, despite having no conjuring expertise, expressed an interest in testing macro-PK claimants.

Phillips was subsequently contacted by two young men claiming to possess paranormal metal-bending abilities: Michael Edwards and Steve Shaw. In fact, Shaw and Edwards were magicians who had been recruited by Randi to pose as psychic claimants as part of a hoax that he dubbed 'Project Alpha'. Phillips was impressed by the feats of macro-PK that the pair appeared to demonstrate during informal testing. In December 1979, Randi wrote to Phillips requesting a report on MacLab's research to date. Crucially, Randi also offered himself as expert consultant magician for the lab's PK tests. Phillips responded that MacLab's work was only at the exploratory stage and it would be premature to report at that point. He also declined Randi's consultancy offer.

In April 1980, Phillips filmed tests with Shaw and Edwards, but was disappointed that most of the apparently psychokinetic metal bending took place off camera. Research with the pair then ceased for nearly a year, until March 1981. By this time, Phillips had recruited a more experienced parapsychologist named Mark Shafer, from the University of California at Irvine, to run MacLab's PK experiments.

Between March and July 1981, efforts were clearly being made to prevent direct physical tampering with the target objects. For example, a glass dome was placed over a rotor; an electrical device was created to measure the apparent ability of Shaw and Edwards to blow a fuse; and small objects were placed in a glass box. Shaw and Edwards later reported that they could easily circumvent many of these controls. The glass dome was surreptitiously raised to enable a gentle puff of breath to turn the rotor; the magicians switched intact fuses for ones that were already blown; and they left a window unlocked so they could enter the lab overnight, open the glass box, and manipulate the objects.

Events came to a head in August 1981, at the Annual Convention of the Parapsychological Association. Phillips and Shafer submitted a written 'research brief' on their macro-PK testing and showed film of their work with Shaw and Edwards. The brief indicated that Phillips and Shafer were personally persuaded that Edwards and Shaw had psychic abilities, but the film received 'extremely strong criticism' from many of the other parapsychologists attending the conference. Randi also attended the conference and pointed out evidence of possible fraud in their film. Shaken, the researchers recalled their research brief and reissued it, having inserted caveats such as 'apparently' and 'ostensible'.

Following this feedback from parapsychologists and Randi, the MacLab researchers immediately tightened up their protocols. Shaw and Edwards found they could no longer produce seemingly impressive PK effects. Finally, Randi decided to reveal the hoax. Rather than contacting the MacLab researchers directly, he publicly exposed Project Alpha in January 1983 at a press conference sponsored by *Discover* magazine.

In a detailed assessment of Project Alpha, parapsychologist Michael Thalbourne argues that Randi unfairly failed to distinguish between 'exploratory' and 'formal' research, that he underplayed the role of the parapsychological community in tightening MacLab's methods, and that the way in which Randi exposed the hoax owed more to 'showmanship' than to science. Randi, on the other hand, has portrayed Phillips and Shafer as failing to have the conjuring knowledge needed for their research. Either way, parapsychologists undoubtedly learned important lessons from Project Alpha. Several praised Randi's endeavour, and the Parapsychological Association resolved in August 1983 that it would consult with professional magicians' organizations regarding adequate controls against fraud. Parapsychologists also started to publish recommendations on how to minimize deception by subjects (see box). Subsequently, many have shied away from testing special claimants, aware of the risks of this type of research, and perhaps also fearful that they might fall victim to Project Beta.

MINIMIZING DECEPTION BY PSYCHIC CLAIMANTS

In 1986, the University of Edinburgh's newly appointed Koestler Professor of Parapsychology, Robert Morris, provided guidelines for minimizing deception by psychic claimants. Morris was familiar with the conjuring literature and was one of those who had advised Phillips and Shafer how to tighten up their test protocols after they had presented their research at the 1981 conference. He recommended that:

- Researchers should be aware of the range of factors that may motivate a fake psychic, including: personal financial gain, fame, power, enhanced self-esteem, and the challenge of defeating the safeguards of supposedly elite scientists.
- Researchers should consult with relevant experts, including magicians, and learn for themselves how psychic abilities are simulated. This expertise should be employed to develop the laboratory's research protocols, and the lab should establish policies to deter fake psychics, such as maintaining subjects' anonymity, and fully disclosing any detected fraud.
- Researchers should also consider the security implications of their chosen mode of research. Those opting to study one or two so-called 'star psychics' are most at risk and should establish firm safeguards against fraud. Those working with numerous unselected participants and seeking to gradually build a body of knowledge seem less susceptible to subject deception.
- For these security precautions and policies to deter potential pseudo-psychics, they must be clearly communicated in advance to the research subject.

These procedures have been employed in several subsequent investigations into macro-PK and helped prevent researchers from being fooled by fake psychics.

Conclusion

Over the years, many people have claimed to possess macro-PK abilities, including levitation, metal bending, thoughtography, and materialization. Investigations into these claims have often revealed evidence of fraud and trickery. There exist a handful of cases of researchers not being able to find an explanation for the claimed effects, but sceptics have argued that such research has not been carried out under the most controlled conditions. Overall, the majority of academic parapsychologists do not find the evidence compelling in favour of macro-PK. However, as a result of this work we now have a much greater understanding of the psychological strategies employed by fake psychics to fool people, including how they manipulate attention, perception, and memory. This work has made a valuable contribution to the psychology of eyewitness testimony and helped researchers devise more rigorous methods for testing those claiming to possess macro-PK abilities.

3

Psychic reading, remote viewing and telepathic animals: ESP outside the lab

From the archive ...

My friend Sandra visited a psychic at a fairground a fortnight ago. She's really worried about what happened. She's quite sceptical about this kind of thing, and had only popped into the psychic's booth for fun. The woman said something like 'some good luck and some bad luck will come your way in the next 28 days'. It was the 28 days that got Sandra's attention – it seemed a really specific statement. Then only a couple of days ago Sandra won £500 on the lottery. It's the first time she's ever won anything! Now Sandra can't stop worrying about the bad luck that the psychic predicted, and she is even finding it difficult to sleep at night. Do you think the psychic really has the ability to predict the future? Should Sandra go back to her and ask for more advice?

(Anne, aged 43)

Those who claim to have psychic ability often appear to use their skills in various ways, including finding missing persons, solving crimes, and providing personal advice. One curious case occurred in 2010 in Australia. The police were hunting for a missing six-year-old girl named Kiesha Abrahams. They were contacted by an Aboriginal elder called Cheryl Carroll-Lagerwey, who had dreamed that a little girl had been murdered and her body had been dumped in the Nurragingy Aboriginal Reserve. The elder led the police to an area of long grass in the Reserve, where they made the gruesome discovery of a torso wrapped in black plastic. The remains were of a missing woman, not Kiesha. Was this just coincidence? Did the Aboriginal's dream reveal some psychic ability or had she discovered the body's location through someone with inside information about the crime? Carroll-Lagerwey did not have a history of locating missing persons; however, other psychics who call themselves psychic detectives claim that they have this ability. Discovering the truth behind such cases is often challenging, in part, because such investigations usually have to take place outside of the well-controlled confines of a laboratory.

Psychic detection

For many years, Sylvia Browne was a regular guest on the American television programme *The Montel Williams Show*. During each of these appearances, Browne would claim to speak to the deceased and sometimes offer information about missing people. In April 2003, a sixteen-year-old girl named Amanda Berry disappeared from her home in Ohio. Her desperate mother, Louwana Millar, appeared on *The Montel Williams Show*, and was devastated when Browne told her that her daughter was dead. In 2013, Berry escaped from her captor and revealed that for almost a decade she had been held only a few miles from her home. Tragically, Millar died before her daughter's escape and so never discovered the truth about her abduction. Browne made several other high-profile mistakes throughout her career, and when asked about them, once responded, 'Only God is right all the time.' She died in November 2013 aged seventy-seven, having predicted she would live to be eighty-eight.

Sylvia Browne is just one of many psychics purporting to use their remarkable powers to help locate missing persons and solve crimes. Perhaps the best known of them in Europe is Gerard Croiset, the 'Mozart of psychic sleuths'. Born in Holland in 1909, Croiset claimed that as a young man he discovered that he could hold an object and psychically receive information about the object's owner. Over many years, Croiset established a reputation for successfully locating children who were missing presumed drowned, and was flown around the world to help solve cases.

In the late 1970s, Croiset's claims were investigated by University of Utrecht parapsychologist Wilhelm Tenhaeff. Tenhaeff was impressed with Croiset and said that he had compiled a considerable amount of evidence to support his claims. However, careful detective work by sceptic Piet Hein Hoebens revealed that much of Tenhaeff's evidence was exaggerated and unreliable.

Fortunately, other researchers have recently conducted better-controlled tests of psychic detection. These studies have tended to employ several self-proclaimed psychics, recorded their predictions in a more systematic fashion, and compared their performance with other groups of individuals. For example, in 2000, criminal profiler Richard Kocsis teamed up with University of New England parapsychologist Harvey Irwin to compare the ability of professional profilers, police officers, psychologists, university students, and psychics. All of the 121 participants were asked to provide an accurate psychological profile of the perpetrator in a solved murder case by completing a checklist of potential psychological and physical characteristics of the offender. The psychics performed worst of all the groups, with the greatest accuracy coming from the professional profilers. Perhaps worryingly, the students outperformed the police. After reviewing related research into the topic, Irwin concluded that no well-controlled study has provided evidence to support the notion of psychic detection.

Few of us have to deal with missing persons, fortunately. Encounters with psychic readers are, however, much more commonplace.

Psychic readings

Many people visit psychic readers for help and advice on a wide range of topics, including their relationships, finances, and career. The website of self-styled 'Britain's best-loved psychic' Sally Morgan, for instance, offers visitors a selection of psychic readers for hire. One is Melissa, described as: 'a truly gifted Medium who connects with Angels to give the most inspirational readings. She uses Angel/Tarot cards and the pendulum.' Prominent on Morgan's webpages are instructions on how to pay for these services. It is clear that this is a profitable business, and Morgan tours the country giving sell-out theatre performances. But what does the public get out of consultations with psychics? Research suggests that they feel they are receiving useful and sometimes accurate information, as seemed to be the case in the archive account that opened this chapter.

In fact, a survey of University of Virginia students found that 67% of those who had visited a psychic reader said that they had found the experience 'very helpful', and 78% claimed to have acted on the advice received. A similar British survey found that 57% of those who had consulted a psychic reader reported that the information given was 'very accurate' or 'quite accurate', and 50% said it was 'very helpful' or 'quite helpful'. Such endorsements are impressive, but is there any evidence to suggest that psychic readers possess genuine extrasensory abilities? Arguably the most thorough, and methodologically sophisticated, research to tackle this question was conducted in the 1980s by Dutch researcher Henk Boerenkamp.

Boerenkamp tracked hundreds of members of the public as they visited thirty-six psychic readers over a five-year period. Each of the psychics' statements was recorded by the researchers and then rated for accuracy by those attending the reading. In all, Boerenkamp and his team recorded over two hundred readings and assessed over ten thousand statements. In addition, Boerenkamp arranged for two groups of non-psychics to give readings. One group consisted of experienced psychological counsellors, while the other consisted of members of the public who were matched with the psychics by age, sex, and educational background. After eliminating vague statements, only about 1% of the remaining statements were judged to be accurate, which was about the proportion that could be expected by chance. Crucially, there was no difference in the proportion of correct statements made by the psychics compared to the two 'non-psychic' control groups.

Given that Boerenkamp's results do not support the notion that psychic readers possess genuine paranormal powers, why are so many people impressed with the advice that they receive? The answer lies in a series of psychological techniques used by psychic readers to persuade people that they know a great deal about their life. These principles are usually unconsciously learned by the psychic over time, and are collectively referred to as 'cold reading' because the psychic does not need to know any information about a client beforehand (and thus is meeting them 'cold'). The main principles involved in cold reading are outlined below.

Stereotyping. Even before a reading has begun, psychic readers are able to make educated guesses about a person based on certain factors, most commonly their age and sex. Boerenkamp discovered evidence for such stereotyping when he analysed the thousands of statements recorded in his study. Young people, for example, tended to be worried about exams, relationships with friends, and over-controlling parents. In contrast, older people tended to be more concerned about health problems, relationships with their family, and their finances. In addition, a psychic reader might base their statements on other, more specific, aspects of a person's appearance, including their clothing, posture, apparent health, and ethnicity. For example, if the person has lots of rough skin on their hands then a psychic might guess that their job involves manual work, or if the person appears overly pale then a psychic might infer that they have issues with their health.

Fishing. This technique involves a psychic reader making relatively vague statements, and then basing further statements on the person's verbal and non-verbal feedback. For example, a psychic reader might begin a session with a relatively general statement, such as 'Someone close to you has passed.' If their client quickly nods, then the psychic might follow up with a more specific statement, such as 'It was someone very close to you', whereas if the client doesn't respond then the psychic might play down the issue by saying something like 'But it was a long time ago, and you are over it now.'

Selective recall. Psychic reading usually involves a large number of statements. For example, the psychic readers involved in Boerenkamp's research each gave an average of eighty-seven statements during each session. When faced with such a large number of statements, people tend to remember those that were accurate and forget those that were wrong.

Population stereotypes. Many of the seemingly specific statements made during a psychic reading apply to a surprisingly large proportion of the population. In 1994, British parapsychologist Susan Blackmore printed ten general statements (such as 'There is someone called Jack in my family') in a national newspaper, and asked readers to indicate whether each statement applied to them. Over six thousand people responded, and in most cases between one-quarter and one-third of the respondents endorsed each statement (see Table 1). Blackmore also asked respondents to indicate whether they believed in the paranormal. Compared to sceptics, those who believed in the paranormal endorsed more statements, perhaps suggesting why believers are more likely to be impressed with a psychic reading.

Table 1 Susan Blackmore's general statements

Statement	Per cent agreed
There is someone called Jack in my family	21.3
I have a scar on my left knee	33.5
Last night I dreamed of someone I haven't seen for many years	9.7
I travel regularly in a white car	24.1
I once broke my arm	16.4
My back is giving me pain at the moment	26.9
I am one of three children	26.4
I own a CD or tape of Handel's *Water Music*	28.3
I have a cat	28.7
I have been to France in the past year	27.1

Exactly the same methods are used by so-called 'platform mediums'. If you visit a psychic reader, or see a platform medium on stage or television, make a recording of the conversation so that you can listen more carefully later. Note what information is being given to the psychic, and consider whether they are using any of these cold-reading techniques.

HOT READING: GOD TRANSMITS ON 39.17MHz

Cold reading allows psychics to give a convincing reading without knowing anything about their clients in advance. However, others claiming psychic abilities have engaged in so-called 'hot' reading, wherein they discover useful information prior to the reading. For one-to-one consultations, psychics can discover relevant information through social networking sites and newspaper archives. For large-scale performances, the audience might be asked to submit the information beforehand, or stooges may mingle with the public before they enter the auditorium.

In the 1980s, the charismatic healer Peter Popoff claimed that he could hear the voice of God, and so provide divine information about people who attended his meetings. Popoff would often appear on stage in front of large audiences and demonstrate his abilities by telling people specific information about themselves, including, for example, their address and ailments.

Sceptic and magician James Randi decided to investigate Popoff's claims. When he attended Popoff's meetings, he saw that the audience was invited to complete 'prayer forms' directly before the performance, and so had already provided Popoff with a great deal of information about themselves. But how was this information being transmitted to Popoff? Randi noticed that Popoff was wearing an earpiece throughout his show and wondered whether he was using this to receive the information. Randi arranged for an undercover electronic surveillance expert named Alex Jason to scan various radio frequencies during Popoff's performance. At the start of one of Popoff's meetings, Jason tuned into the 39.17MHz frequency and suddenly heard Popoff's wife saying, 'Hello, Petey. I love you. Can you hear me? If you can't, you're in trouble.'

Throughout the show, Jason recorded Popoff's wife providing him with the personal information about members of the audience. For example, at one point Popoff shouted, 'Who is Harold?' and an elderly couple wearing glasses stood up. Popoff announced, 'God is going to burn those cataracts off of your eyes right now ... 34788 Foothill Drive?' One member of the couple nodded in awe. Backstage, Jason and Randi heard Popoff's wife feeding all of this information to her husband.

The psychology of psychic detection

If psychic detectives such as Sylvia Browne don't possess genuine extrasensory perception, why are people impressed by their abilities? Once again, it is psychology at work. Let's study a real-world case to understand some of the principles at play.

In 1983, the boyfriend of Mary Cousett confessed to murdering her and said that he had dumped her body somewhere along Route 121 in Illinois. After spending several months searching for the body without success, the police decided to contact psychic detective Greta Alexander for help. Alexander circled a spot on a map where she said the body would be found, and made several predictions, including: 'A church will play an important part.' Officers eventually found the body in a completely different location. Undeterred, some journalists proceeded creatively to fit the details of the discovery to Alexander's prediction, noting that the corpse was discovered about a mile from a church campsite. Indeed, one newspaper ran with the headline 'Psychic key to cops finding remains of slain woman'. In fact, the detective who led the investigation said that Alexander had made over twenty predictions, and that people were focusing only on the one that seemed to provide some kind of match. In addition, many of the predictions were very vague and so could be interpreted in many ways. For example, at one point, Alexander announced that 'The initial "S" will play an important role', which could refer, for instance, to Cousett's boyfriend Stanley Holliday, or a police officer working on the case named Donald Sandidge. This case illustrates how psychic detectives can easily fool themselves and others into thinking that they have remarkable powers. After the crime is solved, the inaccurate predictions are forgotten and the vague predictions reinterpreted retrospectively.

NOSTRADAMUS EXPLAINED

The sixteenth-century French physician Michel de Nostradame is primarily remembered for his poetic work *Les Propheties*. This remarkable document consists of 940 quatrains that make predictions based on astrology. As a result of creative translations and dubious interpretations of these verses, Nostradamus gained the reputation as a seer. Here, for example, is the English translation of quatrain 2:51:

> The blood of the just shall be wanting in London,
> Burnt by thunderbolts of twenty three the Six(es),
> The ancient dame shall fall from [her] high place,
> Of the same sect many shall be killed.

By applying some permissive interpretation (for instance, allowing 'The ancient dame' to represent St Paul's Cathedral) and tortuous reasoning, this verse was taken as a prediction of London's Great Fire of 1666. However, it could equally apply to other historical events such as Queen Mary I's execution of British Protestants.

Sceptic and magician James Randi has created a list of eight rules that aspiring prophets should follow if they wish to be a success.

1. Make many predictions, then highlight those that come true and ignore the failures.
2. Be ambiguous and use modifiers to ease reinterpretation.
3. Employ lots of metaphors, so believers can fit them to many situations.
4. Make double-headed statements ('the fire will be destructive but many will survive'), then choose the winner as matching your true intent.
5. Say God is the source of your messages; therefore, if you fail, critics will have to take God to task.
6. Carry on even if you are wrong – believers won't notice your errors.
7. Predict disasters, which are popular and easy to remember.
8. When 'predicting' with hindsight, don't be too accurate as that will arouse suspicion.

Remote viewing

From the early 1970s to mid-1990s, the American federal government funded a top-secret project to investigate the potential military applications of extrasensory perception. Labelled 'Project Star Gate', the research programme was led by a physicist named Edwin May from the Stanford Research Institute

(SRI) and the Science Applications International Corporation (SAIC). Project Star Gate focused on 'remote viewing' – the claim to be able to obtain information psychically about remote geographical locations.

The researchers began by identifying a small number of individuals who appeared to have remote viewing abilities. Many of these 'viewers' came from a military background and were asked to take part in two very different strands of work.

The first strand involved applied research in which intelligence officers asked the viewers to describe operationally important targets. For example, intelligence officers might show viewers an aerial reconnaissance photograph of a large silo, and ask their viewers for information about the silo's interior. The second strand of research was conducted at SAIC. This work was more controlled, and involved an individual visiting a randomly selected location and attempting to psychically send information about that location to a 'viewer'. The viewer was asked to draw or describe the location, and a researcher would later compare the viewer's impressions with both the target location and several decoy locations.

In 1995, the Central Intelligence Agency (CIA) commissioned the American Institutes for Research (AIR) to review the methods and results of Project Star Gate. When assessing the applied investigations, the AIR concluded that, 'although some accuracy was observed with regard to broad background characteristics, the remote viewing reports failed to produce the concrete, specific information valued in intelligence gathering'. Edwin May disputed this conclusion, claiming that the CIA for political reasons had determined the negative outcome of the operational review in advance. This is not the only time that parapsychologists have argued that the evidence for psi has been undermined by political bias (see box). The laboratory studies were assessed by Ray Hyman (a psychologist from the University of Oregon) and Jessica Utts (a statistician at the University of California, Davis). Both agreed that the

SAIC investigations were better controlled than earlier studies, and that the results of SAIC's experiments could not be attributed to chance coincidence. However, they disagreed on how to interpret the positive results. Utts argued that they represented evidence of psychic ability, while Hyman concluded that the results might be due to methodological problems. The full AIR report, and May's response, can be found online (see *Further reading*).

As a result of the AIR report, Project Star Gate was terminated.

PARAPSYCHOLOGISTS FIGHT BACK: THE CASE OF THE NRC REPORT

In 1988, the National Research Council (NRC) of the National Academy of Sciences published a report assessing parapsychological research into enhanced human performance. The NRC report, by Druckman and Swets, concluded: 'The Committee finds no scientific justification from research conducted over a period of 130 years for the existence of parapsychological phenomena.' Parapsychologists John Palmer and Charles Honorton and statistician Jessica Utts published a response to the NRC report, pointing out its weaknesses. Their overarching complaint was that, although the report was couched in scientific language, it did not present an objective scientific assessment of parapsychology's literature. Their criticisms included the following points:

- Despite its claim to evaluate 130 years of research, the NRC report assessed only the most recent twenty years of work in only four areas of parapsychology, thus being limited to less than 10% of the field's systematic research.
- The principal committee members who were tasked with assessing parapsychology's findings, Ray Hyman and James Alcock, had previously publicly committed themselves to negative positions on parapsychology. So the committee was formed in a way that prevented a balanced assessment.

- The committee had commissioned background papers on para-psychology, but it selectively omitted findings supporting a posi-tive assessment of the field. Indeed, the committee chair asked the author of one report, Harvard University researcher Robert Rosenthal, to withdraw his analysis of the quality of ganzfeld ESP research, which was assessed to be far superior to other non-parapsychological work. Rosenthal refused.

Parapsychologists sometimes complain of unfair treatment by main-stream journal editors and other parts of the scientific and political establishment. According to Palmer, Honorton, and Utts, the NRC report is one example of this bias.

Subjective validation

Some sceptics were puzzled as to why intelligence officers contin-ued to support Project Star Gate if the remote viewers didn't possess genuine psychic ability. Psychologists David Marks and Richard Kammann from the University of Otago felt the answer lay in what they found when they conducted their own remote viewing experiments. During each trial, an individual was sent to a randomly chosen location and asked to send information psychically about that location back to a viewer based in the laboratory. The viewer then attempted to describe or draw the location, and after each trial the experimenters took the viewer out to the target location to provide feedback. An independent person later judged the targets against the trial transcripts.

When the viewer visited the target location for feedback, they tended to see strong correspondences between their description and the location. But the independent judge invari-ably failed to correctly match the transcripts and locations. Marks and Kammann often had to deal with disgruntled viewers, who blamed the judges for failing to identify what the viewers felt were obvious connections between their impressions and the locations. Eventually, the researchers realized the source of the discrepancy. When the viewers visited the location, they focused on any features that matched their descriptions and overlooked any non-matches. Marks and Kammann dubbed this effect 'subjective validation'.

Subjective validation is a general bias that applies whenever a connection is perceived between two unrelated events, and can operate in many contexts, including medical diagnosis and jury decision making.

Psychic birds and beasts: Picking up good vibrations

Research into extrasensory perception has not just focused on humans. The notion that animals may have some form of psychic ability has long fascinated the public. For example, some pet owners believe that their pets seem to know when their owners are coming home, even when they return unexpectedly. In the early 1990s, an Austrian TV company tested a terrier-cross dog named Jaytee who reportedly would run to the porch of the family home in northeast England, in anticipation of his owner Pam's return. Psychologists Richard Wiseman, Matthew Smith, and Julie Milton decided to investigate this claim. They filmed Jaytee's behaviour as a random time was selected for Pam to return home (this would control for the possibility that Jaytee was simply anticipating Pam's daily routine). However, Wiseman's team observed that Jaytee would often run to the porch when Pam was not approaching the house, and they concluded that Jaytee's behaviour did not support the psychic pet hypothesis. Around the same time, biologist Rupert Sheldrake also conducted an investigation with Pam and Jaytee, and claimed that his analyses supported the idea that Jaytee had psychic abilities. Sheldrake criticized Wiseman's study, and continues to dispute his conclusions. The Jaytee debate, which unfolds over six papers, is perhaps a good illustration of what can happen when different methods and analyses are employed to test the same claim, and the difficulties of creating a controlled environment when dealing with living things, human or otherwise.

In other cases, research findings have been more clear-cut. Parapsychologists have also studied mind-reading horses, pets that have mysteriously located their owners over great distances, and animal precognition of earthquakes. Their work has revealed a great deal about how to test such claims, and about the exceptional capabilities of animals.

Lady Wonder

In 1924, Virginian farmer Claudia Fonda purchased a young black filly named Lady. Fonda soon noticed that she would often just think of a command and moments later Lady would carry out the desired action. Eager to discover what was happening in Lady's seemingly telepathic mind, Fonda taught the filly to identify letters and numbers by nudging painted blocks with her nose. Using this method of communication, Fonda became convinced that Lady could read minds and predict the future. Lady was dubbed 'Lady Wonder' and Fonda charged a stream of visitors one dollar each for equine psychic advice.

Around the same time, Joseph Banks Rhine resigned his comfortable academic position as a botanist in order to research the paranormal at Duke University in North Carolina, and decided to investigate Lady Wonder.

The tests were a relatively simple affair. For example, Rhine placed large number blocks on a table, and had Lady stand behind it while Fonda stood to the left of Lady's head, holding a whip. Rhine then wrote a number on a pad and asked Lady to read his mind and point her nose at the appropriate blocks. Lady was correct around 80% of the time. Rhine then added various precautions to prevent Fonda from secretly signalling to Lady, including concealing the target from Fonda, or asking her to wear a blindfold. Through it all, Lady continued to perform well. Despite the tests not completely ruling out the possibility of the horse picking up subtle cues from Fonda's body movements, the scientist was impressed and suggested that Lady Wonder was indeed telepathic.

Unfortunately, when Rhine tested Lady again a few months later, the situation was very different. The wonder horse appeared to have lost her amazing abilities and Rhine concluded that she was clearly relying on signals from those around her.

Rhine's ultimately negative scientific appraisal did no harm to Lady Wonder's public reputation, and for decades she advised visitors on marriage, investments, and career opportunities. In 1956, just a year before Lady died, the magician Milbourne Christopher investigated her supposed psychic powers. Fonda handed Christopher an unusually small writing pad and a long pencil on which to write target numbers for Lady. The magician quickly discovered that he could cause Lady to identify the wrong number by simply pretending to write the number with the pencil. Christopher concluded that Fonda was using an old technique employed by fake psychics called 'pencil reading', and that she could have circumvented some of Rhine's controls in the same way.

Animal foresight

Research with Lady demonstrates the importance of researchers ruling out any subtle forms of communication between apparently psychic animals and their owners. However, such work also needs to take account of the fact that animals' sensory systems differ in many respects from those of humans. Take, for example, the notion that animals use their psychic abilities to predict earthquakes.

On Saturday, 1 November 1775, a massive and deadly earthquake struck near Lisbon in Portugal, triggering shocks that were felt as far afield as Greenland and the Caribbean. The philosopher Immanuel Kant later described how, eight days before the catastrophe, 'a multitude of worms' had swarmed above ground in southwest Spain, and herds of cattle were unusually excited. Kant explained that animals' fear was one indicator of an impending earthquake.

Kant's is only one of many accounts of unusual animal behaviour before earthquakes and other natural disasters. Pet owners, zookeepers, and farmers have suggested that there may be a precognitive aspect to this exceptional behaviour. Unfortunately, it is difficult to evaluate this hypothesis in the natural environment, because one cannot easily distinguish the effects of animals' specialized sensory abilities from any postulated extrasensory abilities.

It is likely that many ground-dwelling animals can detect vibrations known as P waves that precede more energetic seismic shocks by a few seconds or minutes. However, Caltech seismologist Joseph Kirschvink has recently suggested, on the basis of reports of animals' anticipatory behaviour, that there may be several earlier earthquake precursors that are usually ignored by seismologists. These include subtle changes in ground tilt, atmospheric humidity, electric currents in water, and magnetic field variations. Kirschvink argues that seismologists should pay attention to the animal anecdotes and conduct research on animals' specialized sensory systems. By extending their monitoring instruments to include a wider range of subtle physical indicators of seismic activity, seismologists may improve their ability to predict earthquakes. For parapsychologists, the message is to be aware of possible unseen variables that may give the misleading appearance of psychic abilities.

A similar idea may also explain why some animals appear to be able to predict when their owner is about to have some form of epileptic seizure. For example, Toni Brown-Griffin's dog A-Jay repeatedly licks her left hand fifty minutes before she has a major seizure, giving her time to find a safe place before the seizure occurs. Toni's experience is not unique. In 2003, the journal *Seizure* published a survey of sixty-three adults with epilepsy. Twenty-nine were dog owners, three of whom (10%) said their pets alerted them prior to seizure onset. It is possible that the dogs are detecting subtle olfactory or behavioural antecedents of seizures.

The handful of studies into seizure-alerting dogs were reviewed in the journal *Neurology* by Seattle MD Michael Doherty in 2007. Doherty pointed out that few existing studies have employed objective measures of seizure occurrence, and most failed to distinguish between those patients who suffer from epileptic seizures, and those who suffer from 'psychogenic nonepileptiform events'. The latter group show seizure-like behaviour that is triggered by psychological problems rather than by electrical discharges in the brain. These limitations mean that there is presently insufficient evidence to establish how or even whether dogs predict seizures.

Doherty noted: 'An alternative explanation is that dogs are not prescient, and the really interesting data may be not what the dogs do but what the humans did.' He suggests that, in order to identify what cues the dogs may be responding to, double-blinded observers should monitor human and dog behaviour while the electrical activity of the patient's brain is recorded. Investigating such claims of seemingly anomalous behaviour may lead to a better understanding of subtle physiological and sensory processes.

PSI TRAILING

J.B. Rhine's investigation into Lady Wonder is not the only time he carried out research into the potential psychic powers of animals. His parapsychology laboratory received hundreds of reports of psychic animals, including many accounts of pets who were separated from their owner but yet managed to relocate the owner after travelling over vast distances. One case, for example, concerned a Persian cat named Sugar that had been raised by the W. family in Anderson, California. In 1951, the family were about to drive to their new home in Oklahoma when Sugar escaped out of the car window. The family were forced to leave the car-shy Sugar with neighbours. Fourteen months later, Mrs W. was in the cow barn when a cat resembling Sugar jumped on her shoulder. The family didn't think the Oklahoma cat could possibly be Sugar, until they felt a distinctive abnormality on its left hip joint, exactly like Sugar's deformed hip. Months later, the California neighbours visited the W. family in Oklahoma, and were surprised to see Sugar. They explained that Sugar had gone missing seventeen days after he had been left with them, and they had not wanted to upset the W. family by telling them of his loss.

Rhine described three main issues faced by researchers attempting to assess whether a pet has used psychic abilities to locate its owner:

- A lack of unique identifying features means that it is often tricky to know whether the animal has travelled a vast distance, or a similar animal has been misidentified in the new location.
- The pet and the owner might be separated by an insufficient distance, so that by roaming randomly the pet might encounter its owner by chance.
- Third, a case reported years after events occurred might be inaccurate due to faulty recall, and researchers might not be able to locate witnesses to corroborate the account.

In the case of psi trailing, Rhine concluded that the Duke Laboratory's case collection suffered from many of the limitations he had identified, and did not provide persuasive support for the hypothesis of animal ESP.

Conclusion

Psychics have claimed to be able to offer personal advice, solve crimes, locate missing people, and help gather intelligence for government agencies. Researching these claims is often problematic because the work has to take place outside the confines of a controlled laboratory environment. Some parapsychologists have also suggested that political influences have led to unfair assessments of the data. Perhaps because of these limitations, the evidence in favour of applied ESP has been, at best, debatable. However, often researchers have found evidence of subjective validation, selective recall, population stereotypes, fishing, and multiple predictions. As a result, this work has contributed to mainstream psychology, in that it has revealed important and interesting insights into self-deception and deception. Other work outside the laboratory into the possible existence of ESP has focused on the psychic ability of animals. Again, the evidence for animal ESP is debatable. Nonetheless, this work has undoubtedly increased our understanding of the ways in which owners communicate with their pets, and the remarkable sensory capabilities of some animals.

4
Mediumship and survival

From the archive ...

My dad passed away last year after suffering a heart attack, and my mum took it really badly. For months no one could comfort her, until she went to see a medium. The medium somehow came up with Dad's nickname, and correctly said that he'd had heart problems. He also said that Mum had been thinking of changing the kitchen units, which is true. Mum was really impressed by all this. The medium gave Mum a message from my dad, telling her not to feel sad, that he was in a happy place. Dad would be waiting for her, when it was her time to pass. I don't know if the medium just got lucky with what he said to Mum, but he helped her to feel connected with Dad and she's much happier now.

(David, aged 58)

For over 150 years, mediums have claimed that they can prove the existence of an afterlife by demonstrating that the human personality survives death. Parapsychologists evaluate whether there is any evidence for such surviving aspects of the personality, and tend to use the term 'survival' to denote life after death. In modern times, mediums appear to channel messages from the dead, a feat known as 'mental mediumship'. But around the turn of the last century mediumistic demonstrations tended to involve 'physical mediumship', including spirit rapping, speaking in voices, table turning, and materializations. Recently, an unusual case was reported by Erlendur Haraldsson and Loftur

Reimar Gissurarson. They describe how, from 1904 to 1909, an Icelandic physical medium named Indridi Indridason surprised even sceptical investigators with some of his feats. For instance, foreign 'spirits' were said to appear frequently at Indridason's séances. One was a French singer, who sang in a 'magnificent soprano voice' that appeared to originate from 'outside' the medium. The soprano would even sing the occasional duet with a powerful male bass voice that, it was claimed, did not belong to any person present. Few Icelanders spoke French at that time, and investigators took this strange manifestation as evidence that the medium was communicating with deceased foreign spirits. Was Indridason somehow using accomplices or ventriloquism to dupe the investigators? The medium sometimes sang in the cathedral choir and had a talent for mimicry, but despite years of scrutiny he was never caught cheating. Indridason was Iceland's first ever physical medium, but in fact the story of mediumship begins about half a century earlier and an ocean away.

The birth of mediumship

In the Introduction, we saw how the roots of modern parapsychology can be traced back to the mid-nineteenth century, and the Fox sisters. These two young American girls triggered the development of mediumship – the claim to be able to communicate with the spirits of the deceased. During the 1840s, Kate and Margaret Fox lived with their parents in a small wooden cottage in Hydesville, New York. The girls told their mother that they could hear strange rapping sounds emanating from their bedroom furniture. According to Kate and Margaret, the raps were caused by spirits and often responded to questions (one rap for 'yes', two raps for 'no'). After spending several evenings apparently communicating with the spirit world, the family came to believe that the raps were the work of a middle-aged man who had been murdered and buried under the cottage. News of the remarkable rapping quickly reached the surrounding community, resulting in a string of visitors arriving at the Fox house eager to communicate with the deceased.

Imitators quickly appeared on the scene. Calling themselves 'mediums' (because they were seemingly the medium through which the spirits made their presence known), they abandoned the Fox sisters' laborious rapping procedures and developed more dramatic methods of communication. The more extreme of these performances involved a white gauze-like substance (referred to as 'ectoplasm') seemingly emerging from the medium's bodily orifices, and then slowly materializing into the face or limbs of the deceased. Most of these séances were held in complete darkness, with mediums claiming that their manifestations were hindered by light. Persuaded that these strange phenomena provided proof of an afterlife, people began to explore the religious implications of spirit communication.

Within a few years of the Fox sisters' claiming that they could commune with the spirits, a new religious movement started to develop. Eventually referred to as 'Spiritualism', this movement emerged from America's dominant Protestant Christian tradition, and involved both Sunday services and hymn singing. However, Spiritualists rejected the Bible as the primary source of knowledge about God, and instead looked to their personal contact with the spirit world for moral guidance. By the early 1850s, Spiritualism had attracted an estimated two million followers across America, and had begun spreading to both Britain and Continental Europe.

Almost forty years after the events in Hydesville, Margaret Fox confessed to *New York World* that she had produced her supposed spirit raps by simply cracking her finger and toe joints. She later recanted her confession but, to the dismay of sceptics, these belated revelations had little impact on the vast numbers of people who had become convinced that it was possible to communicate with the dead.

Mediumship under the microscope

Some Victorian scientists viewed the popularity of spirit communication as a serious challenge to both the prevailing materialistic
worldview and mainstream religious belief. As a result, several
researchers attempted to discredit the phenomena, with perhaps
the best known of these exposés being carried out by one of
the most influential physicists in history. Michael Faraday was
an outstanding experimentalist whose work forms the basis for
all modern theories of electromagnetism. A devout Christian,
Faraday was also fiercely sceptical about Spiritualism and set
out to debunk a form of spirit communication known as 'table
turning'.

During a typical table-turning session, a group of people
would sit around a small table and lightly rest their fingertips on
its surface. The group would then ask the spirits to make their
presence known by moving the table, and the table would tilt
and turn under the sitters' fingertips.

Faraday suspected that the table's movement came from the
group unconsciously applying pressure to its surface. To test his
hypothesis, he placed sheets of waxed cardboard on top of one
another to form a layered stack, arranged several of these stacks
around a table-top, and asked a group of volunteers to rest their
fingertips on top of each stack. If the table moved before the
volunteers' fingers, then the sheets at the bottom of each stack
would move before those at the top, and, if their fingers moved
first, then the top sheets would move before the bottom sheets.
Faraday's experiment demonstrated that table turning was not
due to the spirits, but rather to the group unconsciously pushing
the table.

Although the majority of Victorian scientists shared Faraday's
scepticism towards spirit communication, a small number of
eminent academics were more accepting of the phenomenon,
including the co-creator of the theory of evolution Alfred Russell

Wallace; the pioneer of wireless telegraphy Sir Oliver Lodge; and the discoverer of the element *thallium*, Sir William Crookes. Many of these academics conducted lengthy and complex investigations into mediumistic phenomena, with perhaps the best known of these involving Crookes's work with the medium Daniel Dunglas Home.

Born in 1833 in Scotland, D.D. Home emigrated to America and began to stage demonstrations of his mediumistic talents on the East Coast during the mid-nineteenth century. He quickly developed a reputation for being able to produce a range of impressive phenomena, including the movement of heavy chairs and tables, and the medium himself levitating and floating around the room. Perhaps most remarkable of all, many of these manifestations occurred under dim lighting rather than in darkness. As his fame grew, Home began to travel the world and staged séances for many famous figures, including Napoleon III, Queen Sophia of Holland, and Tsar Alexander II.

In 1871, Crookes invited Home to take part in a scientific investigation of his paranormal powers. During this research, the star medium apparently succeeded in producing several remarkable phenomena under controlled conditions. On one occasion, for instance, Crookes placed an accordion into a wire cage and invited Home to have the spirits play the instrument. Witnesses reported that the instrument did indeed expand and contract without anyone touching it, and eventually produced a simple tune. In his subsequent report, published in the respected *Quarterly Journal of Science*, Crookes argued that Home's abilities were paranormal but did not necessarily support the existence of an afterlife.

Many of Crookes's colleagues remained unconvinced by the report, arguing that the phenomena had often occurred under poor lighting conditions and had been witnessed only by biased observers. Worse still, many other mediums were caught impersonating spirits, employing accomplices, and using magic tricks to create séance phenomena.

Partly as a result of such exposés and criticisms, some researchers began to examine the reliability of eyewitness testimony for séance-room phenomena. One such study is perhaps the first ever example of an experiment into the psychology of eyewitness testimony. The magician S.J. Davey posed as a medium, invited people to a series of fake séances, and used trickery to simulate various paranormal phenomena. Davey was surprised to discover that many of the sitters believed that the phenomena were genuine, and their eyewitness reports often omitted important information. For instance, they reported that the door to the séance room had been locked, but failed to mention that it was Davey himself who had locked the door (in fact, Davey had only pretended to secure the room). Davey's report on his work caused a considerable controversy, with Alfred Russell Wallace arguing that Davey wasn't actually a conjuror, but instead possessed genuine mediumistic abilities!

The work of Davey and other sceptical investigators did little to dampen public enthusiasm for séances, perhaps because the séance room also offered more earthly attractions (see box).

SEX AND FEMALE POWER IN THE SÉANCE ROOM

Mid- to late-Victorian society was one of repressed sexuality. The popularity of séances is therefore perhaps unsurprising. Mediums were often young, attractive, and female, about whom, in 1875, the Reverend C.M. Davies said, 'we anxious investigators can scarcely complain'. The darkened séance room gave a socially acceptable and presumably thrilling setting for men and women to sit together with some physical contact. It was not uncommon for trusted female sitters to be permitted to search the person of mediums prior to a séance. Male investigators would grasp the limbs and bodies of the supposed spirit materializations of physical mediums. Scientist

William Crookes, for instance, in his early 1870s investigations of a medium called Florence Cook and her claimed spirit alter-ego 'Katie King', was said to be improperly flirtatious towards both. Indeed, it was later alleged that he had an affair with Cook before she was married.

Aside from the evident sexual frisson of the séance room, mediumship had wider ramifications for gender relations, because women were generally more skilled than men as mediums. In the séance, female mediums made themselves the focal point of attention from esteemed male scientists, society hosts and hostesses, and followers who were impressed by their skills. In her book *The Darkened Room: Women, Power and Spiritualism in Late Victorian England*, Alex Owen makes the case that mediumship uniquely allowed women to play a powerful role in a society where their options were otherwise severely limited.

The realization by scientists that many physical mediums were frauds, and that testimony from dark-room séances was often unreliable, caused the majority of researchers to turn their attention away from the dubious world of spirit raps and manifestations, and towards a more dignified form of apparent communication: mental mediumship. There have been several renowned mental mediums, including the Irishwoman Eileen Garrett who established the Parapsychology Foundation in New York, which still exists today. Let us now examine one of Mrs Garrett's most famous predecessors.

James's white crow

Mental mediums claim to be a conduit for messages purporting to originate from the deceased. Typically, such mediums appear to enter a trance in order to channel 'spirit' messages, either directly from the deceased or with the supposed help of a spirit 'control'. In order to investigate such claims, researchers were required to document the medium's utterances, then try to ascertain the accuracy of the messages. The nature of this work is typified by the investigation into one of the best-known trance mediums from the turn of the last century: Leonora Piper.

Born in New Hampshire in 1857, Leonora Piper had her first psychic experience when she was just eight years old. While playing in the garden, Piper suddenly felt a pain in her right ear and heard the whispered message: 'Aunt Sara, not dead, but with you still.' Piper mentioned the strange experience to her mother, who noted down the details of the event, and later discovered that Leonora's aunt Sara had passed away at the moment of the message. Piper began giving private readings as a young woman, and eventually caught the attention of Harvard psychologist, and pioneering psychical researcher, William James.

Piper withstood and even welcomed scrutiny from James and his fellow psychical researchers. In 1886, James made a preliminary report to the American Society for Psychical Research (ASPR), stating that fifteen out of twenty-five sitters had received impressively accurate information from Piper. However, Piper might have been able to glean information from sitters from the area in which she lived. So to make it more difficult for her to do this, the ASPR arranged for Piper to travel to England where she was investigated by its sister organization, the SPR. Further precautions were taken to prevent Piper from using normal means of data gathering, for instance new servants unfamiliar with the host family were employed, and she was escorted wherever she went.

In her England séances, Piper often appeared to fish for information from sitters, and made inaccurate or erroneous statements. However, in 1890, the SPR investigators reported that they also observed numerous instances where she gave accurate factual information about the deceased acquaintances of anonymous sitters.

Piper's prodigious output continued on her return to America; indeed, she claimed to be able to channel Richard Hodgson, a friend of James's and a well-known sceptical psychical researcher who had died in 1905. James's 1909 report on Piper consists of voluminous transcripts of almost seventy sittings in which Piper purportedly conveyed messages from Hodgson. James subsequently carried out various investigations to establish the veracity of these messages. For example, in a communication from Hodgson referring to his friend Margaret Bancroft (who was not present at the séance in question), Piper stated: 'Ask her if she knows anything about my watch being stopped.' James contacted Mrs Bancroft, who wrote, 'I think the watch means *my* watch. We had a number of jokes about the frequent stopping of my watch.' James became sufficiently persuaded by Piper's abilities to state: 'If you wish to upset the law that all crows are black ... it is enough if you prove one single crow to be white. My own white crow is Mrs Piper.'

Taken singularly, such as in the instance of Mrs Bancroft's unreliable watch, the evidence may seem rather frail. But researchers tended to take a 'bundle of sticks' approach, feeling that the case for survival grew stronger as examples of accurate mediumistic statements became more numerous. Thus, impressed by hundreds of similar instances, many researchers concluded that Piper was indeed in touch with the spirit world. Others were less convinced. Critics argued that the assessment of many mental mediums (including Piper) was inherently subjective and therefore unreliable. For example, Piper's statement about the watch stopping didn't explicitly say that she was talking about Mrs Bancroft's timepiece, and so the statement could have been about a friend's or relative's watch. James's contemporary Joseph Jastrow, a University of Wisconsin psychologist, noted that any communication from a deceased person should resemble the character and intellect of that person when they were alive. On this basis, Jastrow ridiculed Piper's evidence for Hodgson's survival, noting:

Mrs Piper pretends to be controlled by the actual disembodied Richard Hodgson. Not only, however, does the latter fail to prove his identity, but he is suggestible, ignorant, inconsequential and Piperian. With alacrity he summoned from the spirit-world wholly fictitious personages, as well as the shades of the known departed; he fell into the most simple logical traps, and through Mrs. Piper's organism exhibited pique and ill-temper at being exposed, – quite out of the role of the shrewd exposer of mystery that Hodgson was. A few whiffs of this atmosphere sends one back gasping to the fresh air.

Is there any way to reconcile these conflicting perspectives? One view was provided almost a century later by British psychologist and survival researcher Alan Gauld. He argued that in the best-documented cases there is evidence for survival *if it is defined as signs of the personality of the deceased*. However, if one allows for the possibility of paranormal capabilities, he noted that it is simpler to hypothesize that the medium is using her psychic abilities to obtain information from the living rather than from the deceased (see box). Whatever the truth about Piper's abilities, it was clear that researchers needed a more objective method for assessing the validity of mediumistic communications.

THE PROBLEM OF 'SUPER ESP'

Some researchers have argued that even the most compelling evidence from a mental medium may not support the existence of the afterlife because the medium could, theoretically, be using their psychic abilities to obtain the information from a living mind or existing written record. A small number of researchers have sought to refute this idea (known as the 'super ESP' hypothesis) by devising ingenious tests where the solution was known only to the deceased and was never recorded.

The first of these tests was developed by British psychical researcher Robert Thouless in 1948. Thouless would use 'key words' to encipher a passage of text. He memorized the key word for each passage, and then invited mediums and psychics to try to crack the code. If they could not do this while Thouless was living, but could do so after his death, this would provide evidence of survival. Thouless died in 1984, and his code remains unbroken.

Parapsychologist Dr Ian Stevenson from the University of Virginia dedicated his career to tackling the issue of survival. In 1968, he proposed a simpler test, which was to set the combination of a padlock or safe with a code known only to one person. Stevenson came up with the idea after reading the tale of a recently bereaved English sensitive, Mrs Greaves, who was frustrated in her attempts to open a padlocked box containing important documents belonging to her deceased husband. Mrs Greaves claimed that she eventually managed to 'make contact' with the spirit of her husband, who informed her of the correct combination. When she tried it, the box sprang open. After Stevenson's death in February 2007, *The New York Times* obituary announced that he had set his own lock test. Stevenson's colleagues at the University of Virginia were then deluged with proposed solutions from mediums. Thus far, the lock remains secure.

How to account for chance correspondences?

During the early twentieth century, psychical researchers began to grapple with the thorny problem of quantitatively evaluating mental mediumship.

In 1919, James Hyslop, a Columbia University professor of ethics and logic, suggested using a 'control group' to estimate the probability that a statement about another person would be correct just by chance. Hyslop was a prominent member of the American Society for Psychical Research, so had access to some of the leading Spiritualist mediums of the time, including Mrs Piper. Using himself as the sitter, Hyslop rephrased 105 statements from Piper into questions. For example, the statement 'You have two sons' became 'Do you have two sons?' Hyslop then asked 420 volunteers to answer these questions, and he used the resulting data as a baseline of the likelihood of a statement being correct. For instance, if forty-two volunteers answered 'yes' to a question, Hyslop argued that the baseline probability of that question being correct was one in ten. A staunch believer in Piper's claimed mediumistic abilities, Hyslop judged that *all* her statements were correct for him. When a large number of volunteers indicated that the statements were not true of them, Hyslop concluded that the results supported the existence of Piper's mediumistic abilities. Subsequent research has found that people are more likely to accept statements that they believe are intended for themselves (as was the case for Hyslop), and to reject statements that they believe are intended for others (as was the case for the volunteers). Although this bias is unlikely to fully account for Piper's impressive rate of accuracy, psychical researchers realized they needed to go further in controlling for possible biases when evaluating mediums.

Another thirty years would pass before American researchers Joseph Gaither Pratt and W.R. Birge devised a more rigorous method to assess mediumistic statements. During studies using what is now referred to as the 'Pratt-Birge' technique, the medium makes statements pertaining to a small number of volunteers (usually without meeting them). The volunteers then rate the accuracy of the statements from both their own reading (known as the 'target' reading), and from the readings of the other sitters (known as the 'decoy' readings), without knowing which is which. These ratings are then compared, and if the medium has genuine paranormal abilities the ratings given to the target readings should be significantly higher than the ratings given to the decoy readings.

In 1994, Dutch parapsychologist Sybo Schouten reviewed almost a century of research using various techniques to evaluate mental mediumship. The results revealed that studies employing methodologically flawed designs (such as Hyslop's) produced evidence to support the existence of mediumistic ability, while studies using the Pratt-Birge technique obtained no such evidence. In 2011, Emily Williams Kelly from the University of Virginia School of Medicine reviewed mediumistic investigations conducted since 2000, and reported her own two experiments into the topic. Kelly found the same pattern as Schouten's earlier analysis. The studies that contained statistical flaws, or that allowed the medium to gain information about the deceased through normal means (such as showing the medium a photograph of the deceased), resulted in evidence supporting the existence of paranormal ability. In contrast, those studies that were more tightly controlled (for instance, only giving the medium the first name and the day and month of birth of the deceased) generally obtained no such evidence.

The latest line of research into mediumship was instigated in 2007 by Dr Julie Beischel of the Windbridge Institute, a private research institution based in Tucson, Arizona. The Windbridge investigators collaborate with a number of 'research mediums' who have been screened and trained at the institute. Beischel and her team seek to replicate in the laboratory the natural setting within which the mediums normally operate. However, recognising the methodological limitations of some other work into mediumship, they place a particular emphasis on employing blinded protocols to prevent bias or leakage of information. For example, information about the deceased was collected by a research assistant who had no interaction with the medium, the medium did not know the identity of the deceased and the bereaved sitter, and the sitter rated the accuracy of the transcript of the medium's readings without knowing whether the reading was intended for the sitter or a matched control person. By 2015, Beischel and colleagues had conducted three studies using these methods, and in each study the sitters generally gave higher accuracy ratings to the readings intended for them compared to the control readings. These results are cautiously interpreted by the Windbridge team as providing support for the hypothesis that the medium is obtaining information about the deceased through a 'non-local source'.

To date, Beischel and colleagues' experiments have received little critical attention, though one area of possible concern is that in order to provide the medium with a 'mental focus', the deceased's first name is given to the medium. The investigators are aware that a name can provide information about the deceased, and take some steps to try to control for this. For instance, if the name of the deceased gives information about the deceased's ethnicity, they try to select a control person with a similar ethnicity. Consequently, the researchers assert that the name does not provide enough information to undermine the blinded protocol. However, rather than rely on presumptions, the investigators could take an empirical approach (as Boerenkamp did), and evaluate the accuracy of information when skilled counsellors (as well as mediums) are asked to provide a 'reading' based on just a name. This would tell us just how helpful a name might be. Whether such a test would indicate a normal mechanism of information transfer that would fully account for the Windbridge findings remains to be seen. Nevertheless, this line of work underscores the message that it is a great methodological challenge to devise experiments to test mediumistic ability.

'I'M GETTING A JOHN ... JAN? JEAN?' PLATFORM READING

Nowadays, people might encounter mediums not around a séance table, but via the stage and television performances of so-called 'platform' mediums. Platform mediums use exactly the same 'cold-reading' techniques as psychics (described in chapter 2).

The British illusionist Derren Brown recently teamed up with the psychologist Richard Wiseman to analyse the performance of one well-known platform reader. Within minutes, the investigators had observed him using five key cold-reading techniques:

1. *Go fishing.* The medium called out various names purporting to be contacts from the afterlife, until a member of the audience said they recognized one. With a large audience, this is easily achieved just by chance.
2. *Make the sitter do the work.* Having hooked an unsuspecting female member of the audience, the medium then said, 'I'm getting five.' After some thought, she exclaimed, 'Yes! Five girls and a boy.' She did the work to make the medium's vague statement meaningful (arithmetic notwithstanding).
3. *Use general statements.* Speaking now to an older lady, the medium offered the following message from the departed: 'How is your knee? And your hip?' Surprised, she accepted both of these statements as applying to her, and didn't seem to notice they would fit most folk of a certain age.
4. *Recap.* Feed back to the audience information they have already told you. In one case, a mere one minute and twenty-two seconds expired between an audience member stating that 'Tammy' was a nickname of a deceased relative, and the medium telling the same person that he was getting the name Tammy, but he thought it was a nickname. An experienced platform reader knows that the audience will forget where the information originally came from.
5. *Blame others.* If the audience don't recognize your messages, claim that the wrong spirit came through, or patronizingly blame the audience member for not being able to make sense of the statement: 'Have a think about it, lovey.'

'Cases suggestive of reincarnation': Stevenson's work

Reincarnation cases differ from accounts of mediumship because the former typically do not involve persons making strong claims to possess psychic ability. However, such cases are relevant to the question of how to recognize a supposedly deceased personality, so we will examine them here. Reincarnation experiences primarily consist of reported memories of a previous life, although sometimes physical or behavioural features are claimed as evidence of reincarnation. For example, birthmarks on the 'reincarnated' person may be recognized by family members as corresponding to wounds suffered by a now-deceased individual. The person reporting past-life memories may reportedly recognize people, places, and objects associated with their previous life. The mode of death of the previous personality is often cited, and in the majority of cases is violent. If the family of the previous personality is seemingly located, the case is described as 'solved'. On average about fifteen months elapse between the death of the 'previous personality' and the birth of the child who reports past-life memories.

Dr Ian Stevenson, who died in 2007, devoted his career to the painstaking investigation of such cases, and his work on the reincarnation question is unparalleled. Stevenson acknowledged the evidential limitations of reported memories of a previous life, cautiously designating these as 'cases suggestive of reincarnation'. He specialized in cases involving children, because typically past-life memories begin to be reported between the ages of two and five years, cease to be reported after the age of eight, and are often not remembered in later years. By focusing on children reporting past-life memories, therefore, Stevenson hoped to minimize the distortions in testimony that inevitably mount over time. He conducted his research by interviewing children reporting past-life memories as well as family members and members of the family of the person who had died. Because Stevenson was trained as a psychiatrist and had written a book on interviewing, presumably he was a skilled interviewer. The majority of cases he documented were no longer 'active', that is, the child had already ceased describing the previous life by the time they were interviewed by Stevenson.

To understand the features of cases suggestive of reincarnation, and of the evidential challenges faced by researchers, let's consider a Sri Lankan case that Stevenson reported in 1966. Unusually, this case was still active when Stevenson came on the scene.

The case of Gnanatilleka

Gnanatilleka was born in the village of Hedunawewa in February 1956. Her parents reported that at the age of one she mentioned another mother and father. When she was two, Gnanatilleka started to speak of a previous life as a boy, and described other family members who supposedly lived in a different town to Hedunawewa. At first, Gnanatilleka did not identify the town, but when she heard visitors describing a place sixteen miles away called Talawakele, she recognized that town's name. She went on to describe her 'previous' father's occupation and the location of the family home, and on the basis of these details the 'original' family was identified. Their son Tillekeratne had died after a fall, in November 1954, aged twelve. Reportedly, he had developed effeminate tendencies prior to his death, and when Stevenson interviewed Gnanatilleka she stated that she had felt uncomfortable being a boy and she was happier now she was a girl. It is reported that, when she was introduced to people from Tillekeratne's village, Gnanatilleka recognized characters previously known to the deceased boy, and did not recognize individuals unknown to him. Both families strongly denied having had any contact with each other before Gnanatilleka started to describe memories of a previous life, and, because of the difficult terrain, travel between the two towns was rarely attempted.

Evidential matters

Gnanatilleka's case was particularly unusual because of the wealth of verifiable details provided by the girl and her family. Nevertheless, some details are troubling. For instance, the concept of 'another family' must be difficult for a one-year-old child to communicate. No doubt Stevenson appreciated that the parents' interpretation and motivation, as well as that of the translators he used to conduct the interviews, could colour the information that he gathered.

Cases suggestive of reincarnation are quite rare, with surveys suggesting that even in cultures strongly supportive of reincarnation only about 1 in 500 people report past-life memories. That figure is even lower in countries where such notions are not widely accepted. Some researchers have observed that in Indian and Sri Lankan reports the 'original' family tends to be of higher social status than the family of the person reporting past-life memories. So, social and cultural factors may play a part in shaping both the frequency and nature of reincarnation reports.

Perhaps because of the difficulty of investigating reincarnation claims, comparatively few other researchers have extended Stevenson's work. However, a few methodological improvements to reincarnation research have occurred in recent years. Dr Jim B. Tucker, a colleague of Stevenson's at the University of Virginia, has developed a questionnaire to evaluate the quality of the evidence in reincarnation cases (see *Further reading*). Intriguingly, two experts in past-life experiences have suggested how to assess the extent to which the correspondences found between the 'original' family and the child's past-life memories could occur just by chance (for example, certain household characteristics such as names and occupations could simply occur rather frequently in the country). Anthropologist Dr Antonia Mills, of the University of Northern British Columbia, and psychologist Steven Jay Lynn, of the State University of New York at Binghampton, recommend creating a long list of descriptors that tend to be reported in reincarnation cases (e.g. birthmark, mode of death, father's occupation). One would then randomly select items from this list to create a simulated reincarnation case, and an investigator would search for a family to match the profile of the simulated case, unaware that the case was fabricated. The ease with which a matching family can be found tells us something about the chance likelihood of a match between a child's apparent past-life memories and another household. Mills and Lynn also suggest that such fabricated cases could be compared with real solved cases to establish whether the latter contain a greater number of idiosyncratic features that are rarely found in other families and therefore provide more compelling evidence in support of reincarnation. This innovative approach has yet to be attempted.

Finally, a few individuals develop the notion that issues in their present life, such as phobias or sexual problems, are the consequence of events in a supposed past life. Readers should be wary of anyone claiming to offer hypnotic 'past-life regression' as a form of therapy for such problems. Any person who has been hypnotized is highly susceptible to fantasies from their own imagination and to any suggestions made during that time. The careless therapist could easily implant harmful false memories, for example of childhood abuse.

Conclusion

For over 150 years, psychical researchers and parapsychologists have investigated whether physical and mental mediumship provide any evidence for life after death. Early work into table turning, spirit rapping, and materializations often revealed evidence of fraud, trickery, and self-deception. Although some studies with renowned mental mediums such as Leonora Piper and Eileen Garrett convinced even some sceptical researchers that they possessed psychic abilities, arguments over whether this evidence signified paranormal communication with the deceased or with the living reached stalemate. More controlled studies that prevented possible sources of error or bias have generally not yielded evidence of the afterlife. However, regardless of the position one takes on the survival question, research into mediumship and reincarnation has undoubtedly revealed a great deal about the psychology of deception, the unreliability of eyewitness testimony, and the challenges of designing a methodologically sound investigation.

Section 2
Anomalous experiences

5
Out-of-body experiences

From the archive ...

Something really strange happened to me when I was a student. I was just lying relaxing on my bed one afternoon when I heard a loud buzzing sound. It seemed to be coming from inside my head. This is going to sound weird, but my body started to feel like it was vibrating, then all of a sudden I was up at the ceiling. I mean my body was still lying on the bed – I was looking down on it and I remember noticing that I still had my trainers on. I was just thinking about seeing if I could 'fly' out of the window, but then my flatmate knocked on my bedroom door, and that seemed to bring me out of it. I immediately found myself back in my body. Actually I quite enjoyed the whole thing. Is there any research on how to produce these kinds of experiences deliberately?

(Julia, aged 25)

During an out-of-body experience (OBE), a person usually feels as if they have floated out of their body and are viewing their surroundings from a different perspective, and they may see their own physical body. Three main approaches have been adopted in attempts to understand OBEs. Parapsychologists have tended to focus on whether they provide evidence of the mind being separate from the body. Neuroscientists have examined what the experiences reveal about how the brain maintains the sense of self, and what causes these processes to malfunction. Lastly, psychologists have investigated the personality factors and cognitive processes associated with the experiences. But what does an OBE feel like?

Out-of-body experiences

The following account was collected in a survey of OBE experiences by parapsychologist Carlos Alvarado. The experienced occurred to a thirty-two-year-old Scottish woman who was training for a marathon:

> After running approximately twelve to thirteen miles … I started to feel as if I wasn't looking through my eyes but from somewhere else …. I felt as if something was leaving my body, and although I was still running along looking at the scenery, I was looking at myself running as well. My 'soul', or whatever, was floating somewhere above my body, high enough up to see the tops of the trees and the small hills.

In 2000, Alvarado summarized over sixty surveys about OBEs. He found that around 10% of the general population has experienced an OBE at least once. For students, the figure increases to 25%, while about 48% of those who are interested in parapsychology say they have experienced an OBE.

Researchers have also established the central features associated with an OBE, and Table 2 (based on the work of American psychiatrists Glen Gabbard and Stuart Twemlow) summarizes the main components of the experience and percentage of people experiencing them.

OBEs are usually described as being calm, serene, even emotionally detached experiences. OBE-ers often regard themselves as permanently changed by their experience, with Gabbard

Table 2 Central features associated with an OBE

OBE characteristic	Frequency (%)
Out-of-body form similar to physical body	76
Same environment as physical body	62
Sense of energy	55
Vibrations	38
Presence of beings	37
Change in the sense of time	33
Saw a bright white light	30
Felt connected to the physical body	21

and Twemlow, for example, finding that 86% of people report a greater 'awareness of reality' following the event.

Australian parapsychologist Harvey Irwin has identified the characteristics associated with OBE onset and termination. Many OBE-ers report physical sensations immediately prior to onset, particularly perceived percussive noises, vibrations in the physical body, catalepsy (body rigidity), or momentary blackout. Around 60% of OBEs occur in circumstances where the individual is physically quiescent, so that there is a degree of habituation to bodily sensations (see box). They can also be triggered by the ingestion of drugs (especially psychedelics and ketamine). For example, a 2011 survey of almost two hundred recreational drug users, conducted by Canadian psychologist Leanne Wilkins, found 76% of respondents reported experiencing OBEs. However, OBEs can also occur in emotionally arousing circumstances, with around 25 to 40% of cases occurring during stress or trauma. Most OBEs end instantaneously. Termination can be triggered by the OBE-er's emotional reaction, such as fear or shock at the sight of the physical body, or because attention is drawn back to the body, for instance if another person touches it. So a weakening of dissociative processes, or the return of attention to bodily processes, appears to be implicated in the OBE's cessation.

HOW TO INDUCE AN OBE:
THE POINT SHIFT TECHNIQUE

There are numerous popular books and websites describing a variety of methods for inducing OBEs. Imagery ability plays an important role in these experiences, and the technique described below is based on practising visualizing your body from a different perspective.

Step 1: Set the scene.
Don't try to induce an OBE at your normal bedtime, because you are likely just to fall asleep. Look around the room, noting the position of furniture and other details. Settle down in a comfortable seat or bed, loosen any tight clothes, close your eyes, and relax.

Step 2: Visualize the space around you.
Try to recall and mentally visualize your surroundings from where you are resting. Think of the location and shape of every object in the room.

Step 3: Visualize your surroundings from a different point in the room.
Once you have a clear mental image of the room, try to shift your perspective and see the room as though you were standing over or near your body.

Step 4: 'Rise' from your body to the spot you were visualizing from.
Try to remain relaxed but mentally will yourself to gently move to that point. Feel yourself moving to that space, and visualize your changing perspective. Then imagine yourself opening your eyes.

Some tips:

1. If you are surprised to see your physical body from a different perspective, you may be 'pulled back' into your body. Prepare yourself.
2. Don't move your physical body. Habituation to your sensory impressions, such as the feeling of where you are sitting or lying, can help to trigger an OBE.
3. OBEs are difficult to induce, so be patient.

The parapsychological approach: Does anything leave the body?

Nineteenth-century psychical researchers used the terms 'soul' or 'spirit' to describe the hypothesized entity that permanently leaves the body following physical death. Similarly, theosophists believe that consciousness can travel in the form of an astral body that is connected to the physical body by a silver cord, giving rise to the term 'astral projection'. The parapsychological approach to OBEs evaluates these ideas.

The work has tended to employ two very different approaches. First, the attempt to measure physical evidence of the mind leaving the body and, second, whether the person having the experience can provide information that could not be acquired any other way. We will consider each approach in turn.

Detecting immaterial entities

Cloud chambers are sealed glass devices filled with water vapour, which are normally used to detect the tracks of radioactive particles. However, in the 1930s, they were innovatively employed by a physicist named R.A. Watters to detect the hypothesized souls of animals and insects. Watters directed a biophysical research laboratory in Nevada, and had developed an 'atomic theory of the soul'. He executed frogs, mice, and grasshoppers within cloud chambers and photographed vague shapes in the vapour that he thought were traces of the creatures' soul as they left the dying bodies. Watters was convinced that his photographs were capturing 'immaterial bodies' but others argued that his reports of his equipment and procedures were inadequately detailed, and his findings could not be replicated.

In 1907, American physician Duncan MacDougall attempted to obtain evidence of the departing soul of patients dying of tuberculosis. MacDougall hypothesized that the immaterial soul would have a measurable weight, so a patient would get lighter as the soul left their body when life ended. As patients neared death, their hospital beds were wheeled onto large scales, and MacDougall reported that patients lost an average of twenty-one grams at the time of death. However, the experiments did not control for loss of water vapour and bodily fluids at the time of death. This, together with some uncertainty about the precise moment of death, may have contributed to the subsequent failure to replicate MacDougall's findings.

Several researchers have taken a similar approach, and tried to assess whether the hypothesized immaterial entity has some effect on the physical world. Probably the best-known investigation of this type was conducted in 1978 by Robert Morris. At that time, Morris was teaching at the University of California, in Santa Barbara. He conducted a series of studies with Stuart 'Blue' Harary, an undergraduate psychology student at Duke University who claimed to have OBEs at will. The idea was to test whether humans and animals could detect when Harary 'visited' them during an OBE, while he was physically located in a separate building.

In one of Morris's studies, a kitten that had bonded with Harary acted as the detector. The floor of the laboratory was marked into a grid formed of twenty-four numbered squares, each ten inches by ten inches. The kitten was placed on the grid.

During experimental OBE periods, Harary was instructed to 'visit' the kitten during his OBE. Two measures of kitten behaviour were taken: number of squares entered per 100 seconds, and number of meows per 100 seconds. The kitten's behaviour during OBE periods was compared with its behaviour in control periods, and the experimenters who measured the kitten's activity did so unaware of whether it was an experimental or control period. In one study, the kitten miaowed significantly less during OBE periods compared to control periods. However, overall, the series of studies did not obtain consistent signs that the detectors were responding to Harary's visits, and Morris concluded that no evidence of the presence of an extended aspect of the self had been found.

In short, although some claim that evidence of the soul exists, the findings are inconsistent and unreliable.

The paranormal acquisition of information

OBE-ers occasionally claim to have seen or heard information that they could not have perceived had they been located within their physical body. A few studies have tested this aspect of OBEs. The best known of these was conducted in 1968 by American parapsychologist Charles Tart, of the University of California, Davis. Tart used a sleep laboratory to monitor the brain electrical activity (EEG) of 'Miss Z', who claimed to have spontaneous OBEs two to four times per week, as she slept. Tart monitored Miss Z for four nights in the sleep laboratory. Once wired up to the EEG monitor, she could sit up no more than two feet, which Tart reported would not permit her to observe the OBE target that he had placed on a shelf about five feet above her head. Each night, once Miss Z was wired up, Tart selected a five-digit random number to act as target and placed it on the shelf. He attempted not to give her any cues about the target number. On awakening from the final night of testing, Miss Z reported that she had had an OBE and she correctly described the target number. However, Tart observed a great deal of artefact (noise) in the EEG signal at the time Miss Z claimed to have her OBE. Physical movement can cause this kind of interference. On investigation, Tart subsequently found that under certain lighting conditions the target number could be reflected on the case of a clock mounted higher on the wall above the shelf. Tart felt this was an unlikely explanation for how Miss Z could have seen the number through normal perception, but he stopped short of concluding that a paranormal effect had been found.

However, other researchers have failed to follow up on this work, and so there is not yet consistent evidence of anomalous information acquisition during OBEs.

The neuroscience approach

Prior to conducting brain surgery, neurosurgeons often apply direct electrical stimulation to the brain of a conscious patient to identify and avoid damage to areas that are associated with vital functions such as speech and motor control. In the 1930s, Canadian neurosurgeon Wilder Penfield was preparing to operate on an epileptic patient and was exploring the functions of different areas of the patient's brain. Once, when Penfield was stimulating the temporal lobe, his patient exclaimed, 'Oh God! I am leaving my body.'

Decades later, with more advanced instruments, neurosurgeon Olaf Blanke reported in *Nature* (2002) what happened when he and his team in Switzerland stimulated the right angular gyrus (part of the temporal lobe) of an epileptic patient. At low levels of stimulation, she reported vestibular feelings of 'sinking into the bed' or 'falling from a height'. As the amplitude of the current was increased, she reported an OBE: 'I see myself lying in bed, from above.' Further stimulation repeatedly elicited out-of-body experiences, as well as various experiences of visual bodily distortions and of perceived (but not actual) bodily movements. Blanke concluded that normally the temporal lobe functions to integrate somatosensory and vestibular information but this function had been disrupted by the electrical stimulation, triggering the patient's OBE and other anomalous bodily experiences.

Less invasive techniques have also implicated the temporal lobe in anomalous bodily experiences. Canadian neuroscientist Michael Persinger reports that applying brief pulses of strong magnetic fields to the temporal lobe region can induce sensed presences, perceived body distortions, and OBEs. Temporal lobe epileptics also tend to report anomalous bodily experiences.

To date, most of these investigations have been conducted on patients by clinicians and neuroscientists. The researchers have concluded that pathophysiology disrupts activity in the temporo-parietal region of the brain. This region is normally responsible for integrating somatosensory and vestibular feedback, and disruption can lead to anomalous bodily experiences, including OBEs. However, OBEs can also occur in individuals without any obvious pathophysiology. In 2013, a team led by Jason Braithwaite of the University of Birmingham investigated what might trigger OBEs in a normal population. He suspected that hyperexcitability in the visual cortex could be a contributory factor in non-pathological OBEs. Cortical hyperexcitability was measured by administering pattern-glare tests to OBE-ers and non-OBE-ers. These tests use high-contrast striped images of different frequencies that some people find uncomfortable to view, which can cause migraines in the sensitive, and may trigger seizures in epileptics. Braithwaite found that, compared to non-OBE-ers, the OBE-ers reported significantly more discomfort, visual illusions, and distortions when viewing the mid-frequency pattern gratings. So the OBE-ers showed signs of cortical hyperexcitability, leading Braithwaite to conclude that some healthy individuals may have a 'neural vulnerability' that predisposes them to certain kinds of hallucinatory experiences, including OBEs. Further pointers as to the origins of OBEs come from research by psychologists.

The psychological approach

Like neuroscientists, psychologists start with the assumption that the OBE is an imaginal experience. Two principal methods have been employed to try to establish the psychological processes involved in producing these experiences. One uses tasks and questionnaires to identify individual differences in the cognitive capabilities and psychological profile of OBE-ers compared to those who have never had an OBE. The second plays perceptual 'tricks' on the brain to elicit OBE-like sensations. Although a comprehensive psychological theory of OBEs has not yet been developed, each of these methods provides further 'clues' that may increase understanding not only of out-of-body experiences, but also of how neurological and psychological processes normally function to provide an integrated and continuous sense of self as being located within our bodies.

Individual difference measures

As the OBE involves the experience of a different visual perspective of the body and surrounding environment, some researchers have compared the imagery ability of OBE-ers and non-OBE-ers. In 1983, psychologists Anne Cook and Harvey Irwin asked OBE-ers and non-OBE-ers to consider a three-dimensional model of a room that contained a block-letter 'F' in the centre of the floor. They were then asked to look at a series of perspective drawings depicting what the 'F' would look like from different positions in the room, and had to identify rapidly and accurately which drawing corresponded to which viewing point. The researchers found that the OBE-ers displayed superior ability at this task.

This finding is consistent with parapsychologist Susan Blackmore's theory of the OBE, which proposes that, under certain stressful or disorienting circumstances, the cognitive system's normal model of reality may be disrupted so that a bird's-eye-view representation of the environment is instead selected. Those who are better able to imagine such a viewpoint would be more likely to see their body from above. However, Blackmore's theory does not explain why the experient feels that their self is literally outside their physical body.

Some progress in answering this question has come from work published in 2013 by psychologist Jason Braithwaite. Braithwaite devised a novel perspective-taking task that he argued more closely represented the kind of phenomenological viewpoint that is typically reported in OBEs. Eight different pictures were created of a human female avatar, seen from either above her head or below her feet, and rotated to be facing either in the same direction as the viewer or in the opposite direction. The avatar wore a glove and bracelet on one wrist, and Braithwaite's participants were asked to look at a series of avatar images, imagine themselves to be in the figure's body position, and quickly say whether the glove and bracelet were worn on the right or left wrist.

In order to succeed at this task, the viewer has to perform a mental body rotation to match their perspective with that of the avatar. Braithwaite found that those participants who had previously reported OBEs performed the task much more accurately and quickly than the non-OBE-ers. He also found that, while all participants reported previous experience of a small number of anomalous bodily experiences, only the OBE-ers reported significantly elevated scores on a questionnaire measure of 'derealization' (a feeling of disconnection between the bodily self and one's own surroundings). Putting these findings together, Braithwaite proposes a psychological model of OBEs in which OBE-ers have a bias (some would say skill) in perspective-taking ability, which, when combined with a temporary feeling of disconnection with the environment, weakens the normally stable sense of self and can cause an OBE.

Another OBE model, presented by parapsychologist Harvey Irwin, derives from related work focusing on the reportedly realistic feeling of the OBE. Using a variety of questionnaires, psychologists have identified a group of cognitive factors that are consistently associated with the experience of OBEs: dissociation (a detachment from reality), fantasy proneness (a tendency to confuse fantasy and reality), hypnotic susceptibility (ease of hypnotizability), and absorption (a tendency to become absorbed in mental imagery). These overlap in the sense that a person scoring high on these factors is thought to be adept at becoming engrossed in an experience. Harvey Irwin's OBE model proposes that there are two principal routes to an out-of-body episode. First, if a person habituates to their environment and the somatosensory feedback that they normally feel (for instance, the feeling of the mattress pressing on one's back when lying in bed), they may start to become dissociated from their physical situation and spontaneously 'flip' into another cognitive model in which the sense of self is no longer tied to the physical body. This might account for those cases in which OBEs occur when the experient is physically quiescent. Other individuals, who have a need for absorbing experiences and have tendencies towards depersonalization, may experience a detachment of the self from the body, particularly under stress, as a coping mechanism. This route may explain OBEs that occur when a physical or psychological threat is perceived by the experient. Both of Irwin's proposed routes to the OBE would be facilitated by the propensity to become engrossed in an experience.

Converging evidence on how the brain may create OBEs comes from psychologists who have discovered how to create bizarre bodily illusions.

Perceptual illusions

Peter Sellers's *Dr Strangelove* character was an ex-Nazi scientist who suffered from 'alien hand syndrome': his arm seemed to have a will of its own and in his case made Nazi salutes at inconvenient times. While this is a real but rare syndrome, it is actually surprisingly easy to trick the brain into losing the sense of ownership of part of the body, or conversely to make a person feel that a fake limb 'belongs' to their own body. Psychologists generate these illusions of embodiment or disembodiment by giving false feedback about what appears to be a part of one's body, or by showing a part of one's body from a third-person perspective. The best known of these perceptual tricks is the 'rubber-hand' illusion.

There are many variations of the rubber-hand illusion, some high-tech using virtual-reality goggles, and some low-tech involving mirrors. But the most basic set-up (which you can try yourself if you can obtain a realistic fake hand) is shown in figures 1a and 1b. The participant sits at a table and places their right forearm and hand on the table behind a panel (such as a large book) so they can't see it. To the left of the panel, and therefore in view of the participant, a fake right hand is laid on the table, and a cloth or sleeve is draped between it and the participant's right shoulder, to conceal the gap between their torso and the fake hand. So the participant can only see the fake right hand (Figure 1a). The experimenter sits across the table facing the participant, and simultaneously gently strokes the participant's actual right hand and the fake right hand in exactly the same place (Figure 1b). After a few moments of observing the fake hand being stroked and feeling the real (but hidden) hand being stroked, the participant starts to get the uncanny feeling that the rubber hand 'belongs' to them as the stroking sensation seems to transfer from their unseen hand to the fake hand. The stroking sensation feels distinctly

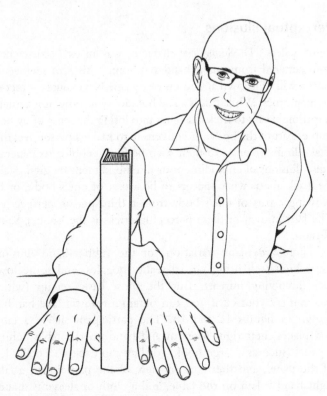

Figure 1a Rubber-hand illusion set-up

odd – there is a slightly numb feeling as though 'their' hand (actually the fake hand) is less sensitive than usual. But the fake hand does feel like 'their' hand, part of the participant's body, to the extent that they will flinch if the fake hand is threatened with a hammer blow. This psychological illusion also has remarkable physical consequences: the participant's real but hidden hand drops about half a degree in temperature, as the brain reduces blood supply to the limb that no longer feels part of the 'self'.

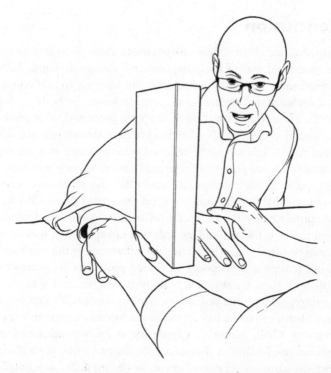

Figure 1b Eliciting the illusion by simultaneously stroking the fake hand and the real hand

This illusion shows how the normal perception of body image and ownership can be disrupted through the provision of false sensory feedback. So sensory feedback is crucial in maintaining the normal sense that one's self is located inside one's body. As with fully fledged spontaneous OBEs, the rubber-hand illusion immediately ceases if attention is brought back to the participant's real left hand, for example by pressing it slightly against the table surface so that the brain receives sensory feedback that 'reminds' it that it owns the unseen left hand.

Conclusion

What has been learned from these various attempts to understand the nature of out-of-body experiences? Parapsychologists have devised some ingenious experiments but have yet to find consistent evidence that consciousness actually leaves the body during OBEs. However, their work is hindered by considerable methodological challenges. Neuroscientists have discovered that the brain region known as the temporo-parietal junction normally functions to integrate vestibular and somatosensory sensations. Disruption to this function can cause OBE-like sensations. Some may argue that the phenomenological characteristics of OBEs that are stimulated by the electrodes of neurosurgeons are different from those that arise spontaneously and unexpectedly. Indeed, it would be surprising if there were *not* differences, as the neurosurgeon's patient is undergoing a planned procedure supported by a medical team, knows what is about to happen, and is expecting to report on some possibly strange experiences. Psychologists have identified factors that appear to predispose a person to experience an OBE, including a tendency to become immersed in experiences, feelings of dissociation or disconnection particularly from the surrounding environment, and being skilled at mentally adopting different visual perspectives. However, false sensory feedback can cause OBE-like sensations in most people, indicating the important role that sensory feedback plays in constructing and maintaining our normal sense of embodiment.

How these various factors interact to produce an OBE is yet to be comprehensively modelled. Clearly, no single approach can provide the full picture. Solving the puzzle of anomalous experiences is a complex and inter-disciplinary endeavour. Parapsychologists, psychologists, clinicians, neurosurgeons, and neuroscientists have each provided fragments of the jigsaw. Even more difficult to piece together are near-death experiences, which we will look at in the next chapter. Once again, researchers from several different disciplines have risen to the challenge.

6
Near-death experiences

From the archive ...

*This experience happened while I was in labour with my first child. I
didn't have any anaesthetic, and as the contractions got more intense
I sensed that I was drifting away from my body towards an incredibly
intense and bright light. I didn't feel any pain or fear at all. It all felt
really peaceful, blissful, and seemed so real. Then I heard the voice of
my mother, who died two years ago, reminding me I had to care for my
baby. This thought seemed to rapidly 'suck' me back into my body. I
was immediately back in the room, following the midwife's instructions.
My son was safely born, but I'll never forget the strange but blissful
experience I had. I don't really know what the experience means, but
I'm no longer afraid of dying.*

(Sarah, aged 40)

Near-death experiences (NDEs) are similar to OBEs in that
they can include a sensation of leaving the physical body, but
are typically more elaborate and emotionally intense experiences
that include feelings of bliss and serenity, of travelling through
a tunnel towards a bright light, encountering divine beings, and
even meeting deceased loved ones. What is the nature of the
experience and what might its implications be for our understanding of life and death?

Near-death experiences

In their 1995 book *The Truth in the Light*, English neuropsychologist Peter Fenwick and his wife Elizabeth Fenwick provide many first-hand accounts of NDEs. The following is from a woman named Jean, who haemorrhaged severely after a surgical procedure:

> I recall floating in a very bright tunnel, everything seemed so calm and peaceful. At the end of the tunnel my father, who had died three years previously, was holding out his hand and calling me to come ... the feeling of calmness was indescribable ... I stopped floating a few feet before I reached my father and then I heard someone calling me. I turned and saw his face at the other end of the tunnel. It was Fabio [Jean's lover].
> (p.105)

NDEs are also comparable to OBEs in that they are often blissful, vividly recalled, and transformative experiences of disembodiment. However, NDEs differ in that they are relatively rare experiences, and they are typically phenomenologically more elaborate than OBEs. There is also something about NDEs that is counter-intuitive and often overlooked: one does not have to actually *be* near death to have a near-death experience.

In 1990, Dr Justine Owens and colleagues at the University of Virginia reported in *The Lancet* their investigation of the medical records of fifty-eight NDE patients. Thirty of the patients had not been in any danger of dying, although most of them thought that they were. Similarly, Gabbard and Twemlow described such an NDE in a 1991 paper in the *Journal of Near-Death Studies*. A group of trainee marines were passing a hand grenade between them when one nervous young recruit fumbled and dropped it. He was horrified to see the pin fall out as the grenade hit the ground, and he froze in terror. He then felt himself travelling through the top of his head towards the ceiling, entering a tunnel, and moving towards an indescribably bright light. A loving figure beckoned to him from the light, and his life seemed to flash before his eyes. Suddenly, he realized that the grenade had not exploded and he felt himself 'sucked' back into his body. With some amusement, the sergeant training the recruits picked up the grenade and explained that it was just a dummy.

Conversely, many patients who are revived from 'death' do not report NDEs. A landmark study published in *The Lancet* in 2001, led by Dutch cardiologist Pim van Lommel, surveyed 344 consecutive cardiac arrest patients who had been successfully resuscitated. Only 62 patients (18%) had some recollection of the time they were 'dead', of whom 47 (12% of the total) recollected at least one of the 'core' elements of the NDE experience (see box).

Cross-cultural studies have found few differences in the content of the NDE experience that could not be accounted for by the experient's attempt to interpret and verbalize an ineffable experience. For instance, a 1986 survey of Indian and American NDEs by Satwant Pasricha and Ian Stevenson found that 62% of the Indian experients reported being 'sent back' to their bodies on account of an administrative error. In contrast, none of the American cases contained this feature. There is also evidence from a 2010 study of deathbed visions in India, by S.P. Muthumana and colleagues, that religious affiliation may shape the content of end-of-life dreams and visions. Van Lommel's follow-up interviews with NDE-ers, two and eight years later, demonstrated the lasting impact of the experience. Compared to a control group, the NDE-ers had reduced fear of death, had greater belief in life after death, and a greater sense of life's inner meaning, and described themselves as more loving and more accepting of others.

Like OBEs, attempts to understand NDEs arise from different disciplines. Some parapsychologists believe that NDEs may reveal insights into mind–body dualism and the possible survival of consciousness after physical death. In contrast, neuroscientists and psychologists regard NDEs as hallucinatory experiences that tell us something about how the brain functions. Each will be considered in turn.

DEFINING THE NDE

In 1975, Georgia physician and psychologist Dr Raymond Moody published his book *Life After Life*, in which he coined the term near-death experience. Based on case studies of individuals who had reported unusual experiences after having been revived from 'clinical death', Moody listed fifteen features that had regularly been reported, though each individual NDE might have only some of these features.

The variety of features, and potential for overlap with OBE experiences, led University of Connecticut professor Kenneth Ring to develop a more rigorous definition of NDE. Ring refined Moody's list into five features that make up the 'core' NDE experience: feelings of peace; body separation (OBE); entering the darkness; seeing the light; and entering the light. Ring created a 'Weighted Core Experience Index' with scores ranging from zero to twenty-nine, and defined the 'core experience' as a score of six or over. Subsequently, in 1983, Bruce Greyson, a University of Virginia professor of psychiatry, further refined the scale into sixteen items forming four clusters measuring emotions, cognition, paranormal features, and transcendental aspects. A person has to score seven or over on Greyson's 'Near-Death Experience Scale' to qualify as having had an NDE. Greyson suggests his scale may be clinically useful in differentiating NDE experients from those suffering from non-specific stress responses and organic brain syndromes. Several other classification systems exist, so there is no single fixed definition of the NDE, and this may hinder progress in NDE research.

The parapsychological approach

Some researchers believe that NDEs offer evidence of life after death. This approach is popular with the public, as reflected in the fact that American neurosurgeon Eben Alexander's account of his own NDE, boldly entitled *Proof of Heaven*, reached number two in *The New York Times* non-fiction best-sellers list in 2012. Other researchers, such as neuropsychologist Peter Fenwick and Sam Parnia, State University of New York at Stony Brook assistant professor of medicine, feel the experiences may not necessarily prove the afterlife but do demand new models of consciousness.

Two lines of evidence have been proposed in support of this idea. The first are accounts of paranormal acquisition of information during the experience that may indicate an immaterial aspect of consciousness that separates from the body near death. Second, it has been argued that NDEs are vivid and complex experiences that occur in the absence of measurable brain activity, implying some independence of consciousness from the physical brain. We will consider each hypothesis in turn.

Paranormal perception

Several anecdotal accounts have been reported of individuals obtaining accurate information while having an NDE. Van Lommel, for instance, describes a coma patient whose dentures were removed during resuscitation attempts. He was transferred to intensive care and, after regaining consciousness, correctly identified the nurse who had removed his dentures and described how she had put them in a drawer. Then there is the well-known case of Maria, a Seattle hospital patient who was reported to have correctly identified the location and description of a tennis shoe on a third-floor window ledge, which could not have been seen from her room. Researchers who have tried to investigate these anecdotal reports, such as Susan Blackmore and Hayden

Ebbern and colleagues from Simon Fraser University, in British Columbia, have found that independent corroboration of the reported events is often lacking.

A proper evaluation of the paranormal perception hypothesis involves controlled studies, where target information is concealed in a location such as above head height in an operating theatre. Resuscitated patients who felt that they left their body as part of an NDE are asked whether they perceived the target. Six studies have employed this method. In three, no NDEs were reported by the revived patients. One study, reported by Sam Parnia in 2001, found four NDE-ers but none had an OBE. And in the five-year study reported in 2004 by British intensive-care nurse Penny Sartori, fifteen patients reported NDEs, eight of whom had OBEs, but none were able to view the concealed targets. Most recently, in the December 2014 issue of the journal *Resuscitation*, Parnia reported the results of an extensive prospective study into NDEs in cardiac arrest patients from fifteen hospitals in the USA, Austria, and the UK. Known as the AWARE study (AWAreness during REsuscitation), this is the largest study of its kind. It took seven years to conduct, and involved over a thousand shelves being installed above head height in critical and acute medical wards. To test claims of visual awareness during unconsciousness, various visual symbols were placed on the shelves. Of 2,040 cardiac arrest events, 140 survivors went on to be interviewed for the study. No evidence was found that any of the survivors had perceived the concealed symbols while unconscious; indeed, only two survivors reported any apparent memories associated with their resuscitation. One of these accounts came from a patient who correctly described some of the resuscitation procedures that had been administered to him, and Parnia and colleagues suggested that this account was a 'verifiable period of conscious awareness during which time cerebral function was not expected'. However, the patient's descriptions could have been based on information obtained after he regained consciousness, or on his knowledge of generic aspects of resuscitation procedures. Parnia and colleagues do not state in the paper whether they evaluated these alternative explanations. Unfortunately, many journalists ignored the failure to obtain any evidence of unconscious awareness on the planned measure, and misleadingly reported that paranormal perception *had* been found in this study. In conclusion, there is as yet no objectively verifiable evidence of paranormal perception during controlled NDE studies.

Consciousness after clinical death

Researchers seeking to argue that NDEs occur despite the brain being 'dead' face two main obstacles.

If researchers want to argue that NDEs are evidence of consciousness after clinical death, it is clearly critical to establish that clinical death has occurred. Death is a process, not an all-or-nothing phenomenon. If the heart stops beating, the brain can continue functioning for a time if provided with an oxygenated blood supply. However, information on brain activity is not always available during medical crises. If a patient suffers cardiac arrest, attention is focused on giving cardiopulmonary resuscitation (CPR), not on attaching electrodes to the scalp (EEG) to determine levels of brain electrical activity. Furthermore, scalp EEG is most sensitive to cortical (surface) brain activity, and is less able to detect electrical activity within deeper brain structures. So, even if EEG monitoring has occurred, a 'flat' EEG does not necessarily indicate a 'silent' or inactive brain. Yet for many researchers the significance of the NDE derives from the assumption that the NDE is an elaborate and vivid experience that occurs in the complete absence of brain activity. In an attempt to overcome this problem, van Lommel defines clinical death as: 'a period of unconsciousness caused by insufficient blood supply to the brain'. He notes that, if CPR does not commence within five to ten minutes, brain damage will be irreparable and the patient will die. However, all the patients in van Lommel's study did receive CPR and most were resuscitated within ten minutes, so their brains did receive blood and oxygen. He does not report EEG measures for the patients in his own study, so we can't tell whether or not brain activity continued during unconsciousness. Therefore, although some of van Lommel's patients recalled NDEs, the precise neurophysiological correlates of their experience are more difficult to determine.

A second challenge is that a person who is revived from death, however it is defined, can only give their verbal report of any near-death experience upon awakening. It is therefore difficult to be certain that the NDE occurred at the time of 'death' rather than during the period of recovery of vital bodily functions and eventual return to consciousness. While it might be instructive to take a functional magnetic resonance imaging (fMRI) scan of a person as they have an NDE, there are considerable practical obstacles to such an endeavour. It is also presently difficult to establish how many of those who have been resuscitated but did not report an NDE have simply forgotten their experience, much as we often forget our dreams.

In sum, the few studies that have attempted to establish whether there is evidence of paranormal perception during clinical death have failed to find such evidence. Progress in understanding whether consciousness persists after clinical death is hampered by considerable practical difficulties, including the rarity of such cases. Other researchers have sought to understand NDEs in terms of biological processes in the brain.

The neurobiological approach

Researchers such as parapsychologist Susan Blackmore have suggested that aspects of NDEs, such as feeling that one is moving through a tunnel towards a bright light, are perceptions resulting from a lack of oxygenated blood and cortical disinhibition in the dying brain. Some circumstantial evidence supporting this hypothesis comes from unusual situations where individuals experience an analogous but temporary reduction of blood flow to the brain. When trainee fighter-jet pilots are subjected to a 'human centrifuge' to simulate the g-forces that they may undergo when flying certain manoeuvres, they can report tunnel-like vision before losing consciousness. However, we also know that severe stress and extreme fear can produce similar physiological effects. This makes it difficult to evaluate the dying brain hypothesis, because the same NDE 'symptoms' could be triggered by physiological reactions to the shocking belief that one is at risk of dying, and by actual proximity to death.

The 1990 *Lancet* study by Owens and colleagues addressed this problem by comparing the experiences reported by those who were, or were not, near death. They found that the two groups' NDEs were remarkably similar except for two of the seven characteristics examined. NDE-ers physically near death were significantly more likely to report 'enhanced cognitive function' (75%) and 'enhanced perception of light' (75%) compared to those not near death (43% and 40% respectively). However, there was no aspect of the NDE experience that unambiguously distinguished the two groups. So how can researchers discover what cognitive processes are associated with actual proximity to death?

For obvious ethical reasons, it is problematic to test directly the dying brain hypothesis with human subjects. However, in August 2013, an intriguing discovery was reported in the *Proceedings of the National Academy of Sciences* by a team of neurologists and anaesthesiologists led by Jimo Borjigin from the University of Michigan. The researchers directly implanted electrodes into rats' brains, so their instruments were more sensitive than scalp electrodes. They then recorded neural activity as the rats were first anaesthetized and then 'euthanized' (killed).

Before the rats were anaesthetized, the researchers observed the normal neural correlates of consciousness in the rats' brains. After cardiac arrest, EEG appeared to flatline for about ten seconds. However, there was then a period of about twenty seconds, just prior to final loss of meaningful brain activity and death, when a surge of extremely coherent brain activity was unexpectedly observed. The researchers concluded (my italics): 'The return of these neural correlates of conscious brain activity after cardiac arrest *at levels exceeding the waking state* provides strong evidence for the potential of heightened cognitive processing in the near-death state.' The researchers speculate that this heightened processing may correlate with the 'realer than real' perceptions that are reported by NDE-ers.

While it is clearly a considerable leap from rats to humans, this study is the first to report what appears to be meaningful and even elevated activity in the mammalian brain just prior to death. The next step would be to try to discover whether similar activity occurs in humans near death, and whether, upon resuscitation, an NDE is reported. If so, this evidence would weaken the parapsychological approach to NDEs, which hinges on the idea of consciousness persisting in the absence of meaningful brain activity.

The psychological approach

NDEs have a psychological dimension because they can be triggered by a perceived threat to life as well as by an actual life threat. In his 2014 review of NDE research, Greyson notes that retrospective studies of NDE experients have found few differences from comparison groups in mental health, religiosity, race, gender, or age. NDE-ers, however, are more likely to report childhood trauma, which is a contributory factor to the development of dissociative tendencies (a detachment from reality).

Greyson himself published a study in *The Lancet* in 2000, comparing NDE-ers with a group who had come close to death but had not experienced an NDE. He found the NDE-ers reported significantly more dissociative symptoms, and concluded that the NDE-ers were showing a non-pathological dissociation in response to stress.

Other researchers have considered the psychological implications of NDEs. Survivors of cardiac arrest can suffer from a variety of cognitive deficits, including memory loss, depression, and post-traumatic stress disorder (PTSD). The AWARE study found that 39% of interviewees reported perceptions of awareness and/or memories from the period of unconsciousness and resuscitation. Parnia suggests that such memories might contribute to the development of PTSD and other cognitive deficits following cardiac arrest.

Conclusion

Considerable practical obstacles face those wishing to understand the near-death experience. The nature of the experience means that powerful prospective studies are rare, so in many respects this work is still in its infancy. Parapsychological studies have attempted to establish whether consciousness separates from the body during an NDE but have been hampered by the rarity of relevant cases. The similarity between the features of NDEs reported by those who are physically close to death and those who are not challenges those who argue that the experience is an artefact of physical processes in the dying brain *and* those who regard the NDE as providing a glimpse of the afterlife. However, psychologists' finding of a link between dissociative personality tendencies and NDEs may provide a clue as to why some individuals experience an NDE without being near death. Recent discoveries by neuroscientists taking sensitive measurements of dying rats' brain activity may add another small piece to the puzzle of the NDE.

The latest study by Parnia also reinforces an important pragmatic point. Cardiac arrest survivors often suffer from cognitive deficits. Regardless of whether evidence of life after death is ever found by NDE researchers, a wider realization that some individuals report recollections of experiences following resuscitation may help clinicians, nurses, and therapists to ameliorate the negative impact of surviving cardiac arrest. Encouraging patients to talk about their recollections may be beneficial in this regard.

Whatever their cause, NDEs are transformative experiences that have the potential to reveal new understandings of how we live, and how we die.

Hauntings and apparitions

From the archive ...

I live in an old house, and sometimes at night I wake up and see co-loured lights flitting about the bedroom. It also seems as though the room turns a bit chilly and I may get goosebumps. I sense that the lights have a kind of 'personality', but I'm not too scared. This 'ghost' feels to me like a friendly chap, so I just acknowledge his presence, then turn over and go back to sleep. I know I'm not imagining things, because other friends of mine who've stayed overnight have had similar experiences. It's just one of those things that happen in an old house, I expect.

(James, aged 71)

Often, when I tell people that I am a parapsychologist, they tell me about their own paranormal experiences. Many of these are ghostly occurrences. Sometimes 'ghosts' are sensed in people's own homes, like James's story above. Other ghostly events occur in public locations that have a reputation for being haunted. Despite the popular 'white sheet' stereotype, such experiences in fact occur in many different forms and sensory modalities. We also know that ghostly phenomena are not particularly rare: surveys suggest that around 30% of Americans believe that ghosts exist. Parapsychologists have been examining the evidence for ghosts, primarily focusing on locations with a reputation for being haunted. So what factors might lie behind these strange occurrences?

Apparitional experiences

The founders of the Society for Psychical Research (SPR) pioneered the systematic study of apparitional experiences. In 1889, SPR president Henry Sidgwick and his wife Eleanor arranged for over four hundred volunteers to carry out a five-year survey into the frequency and nature of such experiences, and their work remains one of the largest studies of paranormal experiences to date. Over seventeen thousand members of the public were asked whether they had had a vivid impression of seeing someone, or of hearing a voice, but had no normal explanation for their experience.

The 10% of interviewees who reported an apparitional experience were asked to describe what had happened. The Sidgwicks discovered several interesting patterns in their data. For example, more women than men reported apparitional experiences, causing some researchers at the time to argue that women were especially imaginative or sensitive to spirits of the deceased. More recently, this type of gender difference is seen as evidence of reporting bias: because women are stereotypically regarded as more intuitive and sensitive than men, they are more willing to report experiencing an apparition.

Almost a century later, parapsychologist Professor Donald West from the University of Cambridge set out to discover how modern-day apparitional experiences compared to those reported in the Sigwicks' survey. West's research was conducted on a more modest scale than its predecessor, and involved asking 850 people whether they had ever seen an apparition, or heard a ghostly voice, but could discover no normal explanation for the experience.

Some of West's results were surprisingly similar to the Sidgwicks' findings, with, for example, about 11% of people reporting apparitional experiences, and more women than men describing such experiences. However, some important differences emerged. For example, in the Sidgwicks' survey, many of the respondents reported a 'death coincidence', wherein they recognized the apparition and then later discovered that the experience coincided with the death of that person. However, West's data didn't include a single example of this type of experience, possibly because improvements in recording the time of death prevented respondents from misremembering or misreporting when a person had died.

In 2009, I teamed up with researchers Professor Richard Wiseman and Gordon Rutter to conduct a survey that delved deeper into the nature of apparitional experiences. In our project, over three thousand members of the public were asked whether they had experienced the spirit of a deceased person or animal. Those who said that they had were then presented with a list of the different types of phenomena commonly associated with such experiences (for example, 'The experience involved seeing something unusual'; 'The experience involved hearing something strange, such as footsteps or voices') and asked to indicate which one(s) happened to them. The results revealed that apparitional experiences often involve several different phenomena, including visual experiences such as seeing a face in a haze or the mist (59% of cases); a feeling of being watched by an unseen presence (47%); hearing unaccountable noises such as voices and footsteps (35%); seeing objects move (25%); feeling that one is being touched (24%); smelling something unexpected such as tobacco smoke or perfume (17%); and having apparatus, such as lightbulbs, malfunction (16%).

Although these surveys have helped reveal both the frequency and multifaceted nature of apparitional phenomena, they have done little to explain why people experience such strange happenings. Unfortunately, the unpredictable, spontaneous, and often fleeting nature of apparitional experiences makes developing such explanations problematic, in part, because researchers are rarely on hand to record or investigate the event. As a result, the vast majority of work exploring the possible causes of ghostly experiences has focused on locations that are consistently associated with such occurrences: hauntings.

SEEING FACES

Richard Wiseman, Gordon Rutter, and I recently appealed to the public for any photographs that appeared to contain a ghost. Many of the images that we received can be viewed online at www.scienceofghosts.com. In the majority of cases, it was clear that the 'ghost' was the result of people seeing non-existent faces in the complex and random patterns caused by the flames of a fire, smoke, or even drying plaster.

Our ability to see ghostly forms in random patterns (referred to as 'pareidolia') has its roots in the brain's remarkable sensitivity to faces. This ability appears to be innate, rather than learned, because even newborn human infants spend longer looking at semi-realistic depictions of facial features (see Figure 2, left) rather than jumbled-up versions of the same features (see Figure 2, right).

This deep-seated facial detection system may have evolved because it allows people to quickly identify possible predators. Indeed, some evolutionary psychologists believe that the ability

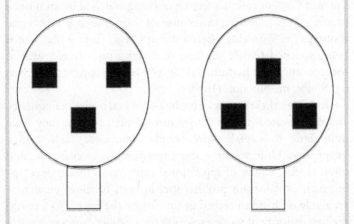

Figure 2 Semi-realistic depiction of facial features (left) and jumbled-up version of the same features (right)

is so advantageous to survival that the brain is wired to see the occasional non-existent face rather than miss a face that is actually there. Such errors (known as 'false positives') can cause people to see non-existent ghosts and apparitions. Pareidolia also occurs outside of a paranormal context, and can cause people to see faces in all sorts of objects and situations, including sinks and car dashboards! The 'giant face' on the planet Mars is probably the best-known case, and an internet search for the word pareidolia will locate numerous other examples of this phenomenon. It seems that an occasional ghostly experience may be the price paid for the brain's remarkable pattern-seeking capabilities.

Hauntings: An introduction

Britain has an unusually high number of 'haunted' stately homes, castles, hotels, and bars. According to guidebooks and folklore, hundreds of people have experienced a diverse range of strange phenomena at these locations, including seeing apparitions, sensing a presence, smelling strange odours, and hearing odd sounds. Researchers tend to be sceptical about many of these cases, in part, because the reports of phenomena cannot be verified and having a resident ghost is usually good for business.

However, from time to time, a case emerges that is deserving of investigation. Take, for example, the Cheltenham ghost. This case was initially investigated in the 1890s by the classical scholar, and founding member of the Society for Psychical Research, Frederick Myers. At the time, a young woman named Rosina Despard was living in a house in Cheltenham. Over the period of a few years, Despard, and many other witnesses, independently saw the figure of a tall woman in the house. The woman was dressed in black like a widow, and obscured her face using a handkerchief held in her right hand. The figure moved through the house following a specific, and highly repetitive, route. Many of the witnesses also heard footsteps when no person was in the house. Myers noted a remarkable degree of consistency in the witnesses' testimonies, and the apparition was identified from a family photographic album as the second wife of the first occupant of the house. Eventually, the occupants moved out and haunting seemed to fade away.

Nearly a hundred years later, the writer Andrew MacKenzie visited the building (which had since been converted into flats) and discovered that the new residents frequently experienced strange phenomena. Many of these contemporary experiences were surprisingly similar to those collected by Myers. For example, in one instance, a cook named Mrs Jackson was taking a driving lesson. Jackson was approaching the house when she saw a tall woman in an old-fashioned long black dress, with her hand held to her face, step off the verge and into the path of the car. Immediately, Jackson braked and stopped the car. Her instructor asked why she had halted the vehicle, as he had seen nothing. When Jackson looked again, the figure had disappeared. MacKenzie interviewed Jackson, who insisted that she hadn't heard anything of the house's ghostly history. Many investigators have been impressed with the Cheltenham case, with parapsychologist Dr Alan Gauld describing it as 'the most famous ghost of all', and psychical researcher Dr Robert Thouless noting that it was 'the best study of an apparitional haunting'.

Researchers have carried out a significant amount of research into hauntings, and this work has adopted three main perspectives: mediumistic, psychological, and environmental. Each of these approaches will be discussed in turn.

HOW NOT TO INVESTIGATE A GHOST

Television programmes such as *Most Haunted* and *Ghosthunters* involve following teams of researchers as they investigate haunted locations. Much of the work involves filming in infra-red, holding Ouija board sessions, and researchers using a range of electronic gadgets. This approach to investigating a haunting is very different to the work carried out by parapsychologists, and some sceptics have argued that much of the evidence shown in the programmes is often less than convincing. In 2005, for example, Dr Ciarán O'Keeffe, then resident parapsychologist with *Most Haunted*, created a fictional character (a deceased South African gaoler named 'Kreed Kafer', an anagram of Derek Faker) and fed this fictional information to *Most Haunted*'s star medium. The medium then regurgitated the information during alleged spirit communications, suggesting that such information may not be from the spirit world.

The mediumistic approach

As a psychologist, Gertrude Schmeidler, from City University of New York, was trained in the scientific study of human behaviour. For example, using blind methods and control groups can establish the effects of expectation and other participant characteristics on their responses. Schmeidler pioneered the application of these methods to the mediumistic study of hauntings.

In the mid-1960s, a family friend told Schmeidler that they believed that their house was haunted. Four people were living in the house, and three of them had reported similar experiences concerning the ghost's location and personality. Curious, Schmeidler asked a draughtsperson to draw a floor plan of the house. Schmeidler then divided the floor plan into equal-sized grids, gave a copy to each of the residents, and asked them to mark where they had felt the presence of the ghost. She also asked each of the residents to indicate the personality of the ghost by choosing adjectives from a checklist. Finally, Schmeidler arranged for nine mediums to tour the house and asked them to use the floor plan to indicate where they sensed the ghost and the checklist to indicate its personality. Schmeidler statistically compared the residents' descriptions with those provided by the mediums, and found a significant degree of correspondence. For example, both the residents and the mediums believed that the ghost in one of the rooms was calm and peaceable. Although the results were intriguing, Schmeidler was unable to rule out the possibility that the similarities were because both the residents and the mediums shared the same stereotypical views about ghostly habits and personalities.

Schmeidler's next investigation addressed this issue, and was conducted in 1968 with Thelma Moss of the University of California's Neuropsychiatric Institute. The researchers found another house that was haunted and asked the residents to indicate where they believed that they had experienced a ghost. Once again, Schmeidler asked a group of mediums to tour the house and indicate where they felt a ghostly presence. To address the issue of the residents and the mediums sharing stereotypical views about the type of places that ghosts might inhabit, Schmeidler asked a 'control' group of sceptics (who did not think they could sense spirits) to look at the floor plan and guess where they thought the ghosts had been seen.

While the data from the mediums and the residents tended to match, the control group's data resembled neither. However, this study was also far from perfect because those in the control group did not actually visit the haunted location, and so wouldn't have been influenced by the visual aspects of the house, including, for example, its furnishings or lighting.

In 1975, Michaeleen Maher and Schmeidler conducted a third study. Again, this involved three groups of participants: residents, mediums, and sceptics. However, this time the sceptics also toured the location before indicating where they believed the ghost had been seen. The results revealed that the mediums' records corresponded to a significant degree with those of the residents, whereas none of the sceptics' checklists did.

In this series of studies, Schmeidler developed increasingly refined methods to control for various factors that could have been responsible for her positive results. Schmeidler argues that her third study supported the notion that some mediums are able to reliably detect where residents have reported ghosts, and are also able to determine the 'personality' of these apparent spirits.

THE COCK LANE HAUNTING

In 1760, a stockbroker named William Kent, and his sister-in-law Fanny, rented an apartment in London's Cock Lane. William and Fanny reported hearing lots of strange noises while they were in the apartment, including knockings and scratchings. A few months later, Fanny died of smallpox and Kent moved out of the apartment. Kent had previously lent money to the apartment's owner, a parish clerk named Richard Parsons, and when the debt remained unpaid Kent successfully sued Parsons. Parsons then claimed that Kent had poisoned Fanny, and that the ghost of Fanny now haunted the apartment. Parsons's daughter, Elizabeth, was said to be the channel through which the ghost ('Scratching Fanny') communicated, and the clerk brought various clergymen, investigators, and even the paying public into the house to witness the ghostly phenomena. An investigatory committee, which included the prominent writer Dr Samuel Johnson, finally ended the controversy in 1762 when Liz was discovered using a piece of wood to produce rapping noises. Parsons was pilloried for coercing his daughter into faking the ghostly phenomena, and was imprisoned for fraud.

The psychology of ghosts

Several researchers have examined the role that psychological factors play in hauntings. For example, in the late 1950s, parapsychologist Tony Cornell conducted a series of unusual studies into eyewitness testimony and ghostly phenomena. In his first experiment, Cornell and assistants from the Cambridge University Society for Research in Parapsychology (CUSRP) took turns to drape themselves in a white hooded sheet and stage a nightly 'ghost walk' in a field close to King's College. Other CUSRP members were stationed nearby to interview any witnesses. None of the seventy passers-by noticed anything unusual. Cornell's second study took place in a more spooky setting, and involved draping himself in muslin in a churchyard beside a well-lit busy road. Once again, members of the CUSRP were at hand to help in case any passers-by 'became hysterical'. Although a handful of people noticed the fake apparition, none attributed it to anything paranormal. In his final experiment, Cornell upped the ante by having the white-sheeted 'ghost' walk in front of a cinema screen while a trailer was playing. The ghost was in clear view for just under a minute. Cornell later explained to the audience that they had taken part in an experiment, and asked them to report what, if anything, they had noticed. The ghostly appearance was not spotted by almost half of the audience. Others reported a variety of observations, including a young girl in a white frock and a white polar bear. Cornell's work suggests that, if genuine apparitions walk the earth, it is quite possible that many people would fail to notice them! Cornell's unusual studies were recently celebrated as an early example of a psychological phenomenon known as 'inattentional blindness', wherein people fail to see unusual and obvious events around them.

Other psychologists have taken a somewhat different approach and examined the psychological processes that might underlie ghostly experiences. For example, in the late 1990s, Southern Illinois University researchers James Houran and Rense Lange examined the role of expectation in hauntings. Houran and Lange took participants on a tour of a theatre that was being renovated, and had them complete a questionnaire about their spiritual, psychic, emotional, and physiological experiences. Half of the participants were told that the theatre was haunted, while the other half acted as a control and were informed merely that it was being remodelled. Those in the 'haunted' group reported significantly more unusual experiences than those in the 'remodelled' group.

In another strand of this work, Lange and Houran examined how fear can create evidence of a haunting. The researchers argued that people often feel uneasy when they go into a place that they believe to be haunted, and that this sense of unease can cause them to become hyper-vigilant. As a result, they are highly likely to notice any subtle sights and sounds in their surroundings (such as a creaking floorboard or slight draught), and attribute this to ghostly activity. This, in turn, makes them even more fearful and vigilant, and so even more likely to notice additional subtle phenomena. This process acts like a positive feedback loop, building on itself until the person becomes extremely scared and perhaps even suffers a panic attack. Lange and Houran suggest that, in a group, such emotional reactions can be contagious. So a ghostly event experienced by just one jumpy person can make nearby folk nervous, causing them to have similar experiences. Perhaps this explains the recent surge in the popularity of 'haunted vigils' as a form of entertainment.

There is also research demonstrating that believers in the paranormal respond differently to ambiguous stimuli compared to disbelievers. Susan Blackmore showed believers and disbelievers a series of pictures that had been degraded to various degrees by the addition of visual noise. Believers were quicker than disbelievers to identify what was in each picture, but they made more wrong identifications than the disbelievers. Blackmore suggests that believers might be more creative than disbelievers, meaning that they would be better able to see forms in ambiguous stimuli.

This work has demonstrated that an understanding of psychology is vital to those who wish to fully explore hauntings and other forms of seemingly ghostly activity.

The environmental approach

Popular depictions of 'ghosthunters' have the investigator using electronic gadgets to scan an area where a ghost has been seen. They appear to be seeking some physical 'trace' of the ghost, even though parapsychologists have no idea what kind of physical trace an immaterial ghost might leave. However, rather than the ghost causing physical traces, the reverse may be a more plausible hypothesis. Some researchers have speculated that those reporting strange feelings in haunted locations are responding to some unusual aspect of the environment. Most of this work has examined the possible role played by two factors: electromagnetism and low-frequency sounds. Each will be discussed in turn.

Neuroscientist Dr Michael Persinger is director of The Consciousness Research Laboratory at Laurentian University, Ontario. Persinger has speculated that changes in geomagnetic fields in the earth's crust could stimulate the brain's temporal lobes and produce many of the subjective experiences associated with hauntings. Several researchers have attempted to assess this hypothesis by measuring the local magnetic activity in haunted sites. This work has yielded mixed results. However, the strongest evidence for the electromagnetic field theory comes from Persinger's own laboratory-based research.

In the mid-1980s, Persinger created the 'God Helmet', to discover whether certain types of brain stimulation result in people having unusual experiences. This unusual device consists of a modified motorcycle helmet containing electromagnetic coils that create a mild (one millitesla) electromagnetic field. Persinger claims that this field interferes with the temporal lobes of the brain and results in people having a range of unusual feelings, including sensed presences and mystical experiences. Many volunteers have taken part in studies with the God Helmet, and the majority have reported experiencing a variety of unusual feelings.

However, not everyone is convinced. Biologist and author Richard Dawkins tried on the God Helmet as part of a television documentary and reported that 'it pretty much felt as though I was in total darkness, with a helmet on my head and pleasantly relaxed'. Other critics have pointed out that the helmet is unlikely to have any effect on the brain because it is generating magnetic fields that are around five thousand times weaker than a typical refrigerator magnet. In 2005, a team led by psychologist Pehr Granqvist from Uppsala University, Sweden, suspected that Persinger's volunteers were responding to their expectations rather than to the rather weak electromagnetic fields. To find out if this was the case, Granqvist conducted a double-blind study where neither the experimenters nor the volunteers knew when the fields were activated. Under these more controlled conditions, there was no evidence to support the effects of the magnetic fields.

While Persinger speculates that changes in geomagnetic fields may produce many of the subjective experiences associated with hauntings, other researchers believe that some hauntings are the result of low-frequency waves known as infrasound. This approach is perhaps most closely associated with the work of engineering designer Vic Tandy.

In the mid-1990s, Tandy was working for a company that manufactured intensive-care life support equipment. Many of the people working in the laboratory experienced a variety of strange sensations, including unaccountable goosebumps, feelings of uneasiness, and glimpsing non-existent figures in their peripheral vision. One night, Tandy was working alone in the laboratory and felt a strong sense of presence in the room. He spotted a shadowy grey figure on the periphery of his vision but, when he turned to face the apparition, it faded and disappeared.

Early the next day, in preparation for a fencing competition, Tandy brought a spare foil blade into the laboratory. He fixed the blade in a bench vice, and was surprised to see the free end of the foil 'frantically vibrating'. Tandy systematically moved the clamped blade to different positions along the length of the laboratory and noticed systematic changes in the degree of vibration of the blade. In some spots, the blade did not move at all, whereas in others it vibrated. Tandy eventually realized that the movement was the result of a low-frequency standing wave of 19Hz that was being produced by an extractor fan in an adjacent room and that was effectively amplified by the shape of the laboratory. Tandy surveyed the literature on the effects of such infrasonic stimulation, and found that the symptoms included oppressive feelings, sensations of fear, chilling, and blurring of vision. The ghost was banished from Tandy's laboratory by modifying the extractor fan's mounting, but Tandy speculated that certain hauntings might be the results of infrasound.

Tandy had an opportunity to test his idea when he heard about a fourteenth-century cellar in Coventry that was strongly associated with a variety of ghostly experiences. Tandy took highly sensitive acoustic measuring equipment to the cellar and detected a clear and significant 19Hz infrasound signal. Although not every haunting will be the result of infrasound, Tandy's theory seems likely to provide a fascinating explanation for certain cases.

Hampton Court and Edinburgh's underground vaults

A few years ago, I carried out a series of investigations into hauntings in collaboration with Professor Richard Wiseman from the

University of Hertfordshire. The studies aimed to examine the psychological and environmental approaches to hauntings.

Our first study took place at Hampton Court Palace in Richmond in London, which was originally inhabited by Henry VIII. In 1540, Henry married Catherine Howard. A few years later, Henry suspected Howard of having an affair and ordered her execution. According to folklore, Howard was dragged screaming along a gallery, and since then people have experienced a range of strange phenomena in what is now known as the Haunted Gallery.

At the start of our investigation, we arranged for over six hundred members of the public to walk around the Haunted Gallery, and mark on a floor plan the location of any strange feelings that they might have. Around half of the volunteers reported strange experiences, including an unusual change in temperature, feelings of dizziness, odd odours, a sense of presence, and intense emotional feelings. As predicted by the psychological work into hauntings, those volunteers who believed in ghosts were especially likely to both report an unusual feeling and attribute these sensations to ghosts.

Our work also assessed the environmental approach to hauntings. Prior to the investigation, a palace warder was asked to mark on the floor plan the location of historical reports of ghostly phenomena. To avoid possible bias, the research team did not know the location of these areas during the investigation. In line with previous studies, volunteers' experiences tended to cluster in the historical 'haunted' locations identified by the palace warder. Additional research revealed that the magnetic activity in the 'haunted' areas was more variable compared to the other areas, suggesting that perhaps the public were responding to this environmental factor.

A follow-up study was carried out in a series of underground vaults in Edinburgh. These vaults were constructed during the eighteenth century, and consist of a series of dank and dark cellars of varying sizes. Throughout their history, people have reported a wide range of unusual experiences in the vaults. During our experiment, hundreds of volunteers were asked to spend a few minutes in each of the vaults and report whether they had an unusual experience. The results were mostly consistent with the Hampton Court study. Nearly half of the volunteers reported at least one strange experience, with those who believed in the existence of ghosts reporting more experiences than others. Prior to the investigation, a historian reviewed the records of the past experiences and established the degree to which each vault was associated with such experiences. During the study, the volunteers had significantly more strange experiences in the vaults that had attracted the most ghostly reports over time.

Our Edinburgh vaults study also involved measuring a large number of environmental variables, including magnetic activity, air temperature, air movement, light levels, and the dimensions of each vault. Although this time the magnetic measurements were inconclusive, participants tended to report a greater number of strange experiences in vaults that were relatively large and dark.

These investigations explored the psychological and environmental approach to hauntings. The findings suggest that no single factor is likely to provide a complete explanation, and that each of the perspectives plays a role in explaining why some locations cause people to experience strange feelings.

Conclusion

People have long reported experiencing ghostly phenomena. Most research into the area has involved investigating haunted locations. This work has taken several perspectives. Some research has examined whether mediums can accurately identify the location and personality of the ghosts. Other studies have examined the role that psychological factors such as expectation, belief, and fear can play in hauntings. Finally, a third strand of work has examined the possible role played by environmental variables, including electromagnetism and infrasound. Some of the most recent research has involved investigating these latter two perspectives, with work in Hampton Court Palace and Edinburgh's underground vaults illustrating the need for a multi-faceted approach to hauntings.

8

The psychology of psychic experiences

From the archive ...

My aunt can predict the sex of unborn children. She holds a chain with a crystal at the end of it, like a pendulum, over the 'bump' of pregnant women. She says if the crystal swings in a clockwise direction it's a baby girl, or a boy if it goes anti-clockwise. She's nearly always accurate with this method – the only time it doesn't work so well is if she is feeling poorly. My aunt lives in a Scottish village, and has got quite a reputation with the locals over the years. Some young couples have even decorated their nursery according to her predictions!

(Joan, aged 37)

Reports of psychic experiences usually involve a seemingly remarkable connection between someone's thoughts or feelings and an event. For example, a person may dream about suddenly becoming wealthy, and then win the lottery the following day. Or a mother may experience an unusual and sudden pain in her stomach, and then later discover that her son was involved in an accident at that precise moment. Researchers have examined the psychological mechanisms that may contribute to these curious experiences, with much of the work focusing on possible explanations for dream precognition. The basic assumption underlying this approach is that most, if not all, paranormal experiences are in fact not due to paranormal phenomena, but to misattributions or erroneous judgements that arise quite understandably out of normal mental processes.

Cognition without awareness

Many aspects of thinking and perception take place outside of awareness. In one study conducted by Stanford University psychologist Robert Zajonc, for example, volunteers were shown several abstract symbols that resembled Chinese characters. They were then shown a series of symbols that contained both the symbols they had previously seen and new ones, and they were asked to identify the ones they had previously seen. Although the volunteers were unable to identify accurately the old symbols, when asked to rate the degree to which they liked each symbol they preferred the designs that they had seen before. Without their realizing it, the volunteers' preferences had been influenced by their past experience. In another study, researchers asked volunteers to pick up two small metal bars and decide which was the heavier. There was only a very small difference between the weight of the bars, and the volunteers were convinced that they were making random guesses. However, the results revealed that they were identifying the heavier bar more often than by chance.

Some researchers, such as psychology professor James Alcock from York University in Canada, have suggested that some psychic experiences might be due to factors outside of awareness. Take, for instance, reports of precognitive dreaming. Research has shown that many dreams reflect people's deep-seated worries and concerns, and this might form the basis for a precognitive dream. For example, someone unconsciously notices that their friend appears unusually pale, dreams about their being unwell, and then wakes up to discover that their friend has had a heart attack. Other research suggests that when people are asleep they often incorporate external sounds into their dreams. This phenomenon is known as 'dream intrusion'. For example, someone might unconsciously hear their alarm clock ringing and convert this sound into church bells during their dream. This phenomenon could cause a seemingly precognitive dream experience. For instance, if someone has set their radio to come on around the time they want to wake up, they might unconsciously hear a news report about an aeroplane crash and dream about the tragedy. When they do get up, they might read about the crash in a newspaper and think that they predicted it during their dream.

I have recently started to investigate the possible relationship between dream intrusion and precognitive experiences. One initial study involved a group of nine volunteers who claimed that their dreams often predicted the future. The volunteers were invited to spend a night at a sleep laboratory. Their brainwaves were monitored throughout the night, and when the data suggested that they were dreaming, we quietly played one of four 'soundscapes' into the volunteer's room. These soundscapes were designed to elicit certain images and involved, for example, the sounds of waves lapping against a beach or birds singing in trees. After about five minutes, volunteers were woken up and asked to describe their dream. The results revealed evidence of dream intrusion, with the soundscapes frequently influencing the nature of their dreams. In addition, there was some evidence to suggest that the amount of intrusion was related to the degree to which they reported experiencing precognitive dreams. This was just a small-scale study, but if the results replicate with larger numbers of volunteers we will have discovered one of the reasons why precognitive dream experiences are so common.

UNCONSCIOUS LEARNING AND CARD GUESSING

Many of the early experiments into the possible existence of ESP involved people trying to guess the order of shuffled decks of cards. Much of this work involved a small number of volunteers making thousands of guesses, and critics noted that, if the decks weren't shuffled properly, the volunteers might be unconsciously detecting patterns in the order of the cards. The idea may sound far-fetched but research suggests that it is indeed possible to unconsciously detect such patterns.

In one study, Stuart Wilson, from Queen Margaret University in Edinburgh, showed volunteers a series of ESP cards and asked them to predict which cards would come next. The order of the cards was determined by a simple rule, and Wilson speculated that the volunteers would unconsciously learn the rule and so guess the next few cards at above-chance levels. As predicted, the volunteers' card guessing gradually became faster and more accurate as they unconsciously learned the rule.

The rule used to govern the order of the cards in Wilson's study would have been much easier to detect than any patterns that may have been present in the early ESP experiments. However, his results sound a warning bell, and highlight the importance of researchers ensuring that such studies rule out the possibility of unconscious learning.

Probability misjudgement

Imagine bumping into a friend that you haven't seen in years. Your friend explains that they now have two children, and that one of their children is a girl. What are the chances of their other child being a boy? When most people are presented with this problem they think that the answer is 50%. However, this is not the case. When your friend's children were born, there were four equally probable possible scenarios:

A)   Their first child was a **boy** and their second child was a **boy**.

B)   Their first child was a **boy** and their second child was a **girl**.

C)   Their first child was a **girl** and their second child was a **boy**.

D)   Their first child was a **girl** and their second child was a **girl**.

Your friend told you that one of their children was a girl, and therefore scenario A can't be the case. That just leaves the following three possible scenarios:

B)   Their first child was a **boy** and their second child was a **girl**.

C)   Their first child was a **girl** and their second child was a **boy**.

D)   Their first child was a **girl** and their second child was a **girl**.

Two out of three of these possible scenarios result in the other child being a boy, and therefore the chances are two-thirds.

People frequently produce the wrong answer to this puzzle because they misunderstand the nature of probability, and some researchers have argued that this lack of understanding can cause them to think that they have had a psychic experience. Much of the work exploring this possibility has again focused on how it might operate within the context of precognitive dreaming.

Let's assume that someone has just one dream each night of their life from when they are fifteen years old to when they are seventy-five years old. Those sixty years of dreaming will result in about twenty-two thousand dreams. Now let's assume that there will be only one dramatic aeroplane crash in this person's life and randomly assign it to any one day. Finally, let's assume that the person will have only one dream about such a dramatic aeroplane crash in their entire life, and randomly assign that to one night. The chances of the person having their 'aeroplane disaster' dream the night before the actual crash is about a massive 22,000 to 1.

Now let's assume this person lives in Britain. There are around sixty-four million people currently living in Britain, and these events could have happened to any of them. Given that the chances of having the 'aeroplane disaster' dream one night and the actual crash is about 22,000 to 1, one person in every twenty-two thousand, or roughly three thousand people, would be expected to have this amazing experience in each generation. Mathematician Persi Diaconis has dubbed this phenomenon the Law of Truly Large Numbers, noting that 'with a large enough sample, any outrageous thing is likely to happen'. In reality, of course, people have far more than one dream each night, and unfortunately there are several major accidents and other tragedies each year. Because of this, the actual number of precognitive experiences that happen just by chance alone will be much higher.

In addition to demonstrating that people often underestimate the chances of psychic experiences, researchers have also explored whether people who believe in the paranormal are especially poor at understanding probability. In one study, for example, psychologists Jochen Musch and Katja Ehrenberg, from the University of Bonn, asked volunteers to complete a questionnaire about their paranormal beliefs, note down their school exam results, and then answer several probability-based questions (for example, 'Is throwing ten dice and getting ten sixes as likely as throwing one dice ten times and getting ten sixes?' – the correct answer is 'yes'). The researchers discovered that the volunteers who believed in the paranormal tended to obtain lower scores on the questions about probability, but that this difference disappeared when they took into account the participants' exam grades. Overall, their results suggest that those who believe in the paranormal might be less likely than others to consider several normal factors, including probability, that might account for their psychic experiences.

Propensity to find correspondences

Most reports of psychic experiences involve some kind of correspondence between someone's thoughts or feelings and an event. However, people vary in the degree to which they perceive such correspondences. Imagine, for example, that you had a dream about becoming a millionaire, and then you win the jackpot in the national lottery the following day. Would you think that there was a strong correspondence between your dream and the subsequent win? Now imagine that you had the same dream, and that the following day you came across a fifty-dollar bill on the street. Do you now think that there is a strong correspondence between your dream and the following day's events? Finally, imagine that you had the millionaire dream, and then the following day you turn on the television and watch a quiz show in which a contestant wins a large amount of money. Is there a correspondence this time?

People's answers to these questions vary, and researchers have speculated that those who report lots of seemingly psychic experiences might be especially likely to see such correspondences.

I recently conducted a study that tested this idea within the context of precognitive dreaming. I started off by randomly pairing up twenty entries from someone's dream diary with twenty reports of major world events taken from a news archive. I then asked a group of volunteers to indicate how many precognitive dreams they had had, and had them rate the degree of correspondence between each dream-entry/news-report pairing. As predicted, those who had had precognitive dreams were especially likely to believe that the pairings contained large amounts of correspondence.

Other research has explored the psychological factors that might underlie the ability to find such correspondences, with some work suggesting that those who report lots of psychic experiences are more creative and imaginative than others (see box). Some researchers have noted that at the more extreme end of the spectrum the ability to see such correspondences may relate to the concept of 'schizotypy'. Schizotypy is the tendency to experience milder forms of symptoms commonly associated with schizophrenia, such as hallucinations or bizarre interpretations of events. However, the relationship between reporting psychic experiences and schizotypy is weak, and it would be unwise to equate reports of such experiences with mental illness. Indeed, Gordon Claridge of University College London and Christine Simmonds of the University of West Georgia argue that some schizotypal individuals are otherwise well adjusted, and that studying these 'healthy schizotypes' may help mainstream psychologists to understand the processes underlying the development of psychosis.

FANTASY PRONENESS AND IMAGINATION

Psychologists have developed several questionnaires to measure a concept known as 'fantasy proneness'. Those who score highly on the questionnaires are often seen as creative, imaginative, and easily hypnotized. Various researchers have explored the possible relationship between fantasy proneness and the reporting of paranormal experiences. Some of this work provides an interesting illustration of how different methods can yield conflicting results.

In 1992, sociologist Robert Bartholomew and his colleagues studied biographical information about 152 people who claimed to have been abducted by aliens. The research team concluded that 132 of these abductees reported phenomena consistent with a fantasy-prone personality, including out-of-body experiences, religious visions, and seeing apparitions.

However, in another study, sceptical psychologist Christopher French from Goldsmiths College in London asked a different group of abductees to complete a fantasy-proneness questionnaire, and found no evidence to support any relationship. Some researchers have tried to resolve these different patterns of findings by arguing that those completing French's questionnaires may have given false answers to try to avoid appearing strange or having an overactive imagination.

Whatever the explanation, the work highlights the importance of understanding how the wider research context as well as the methods used can impact on the data collected and inferences drawn.

Selective memory

The apparent accuracy of a psychic reading can be inflated by clients selectively remembering accurate statements and forgetting the inaccurate ones. Such selective remembering can also play a key role in causing people to erroneously believe that they have had a psychic experience. For example, many people claim to have had the psychic experience of hearing their telephone ringing and knowing who is calling them, even though they didn't expect the person to call. However, in reality, it is quite possible that people are simply forgetting about the times when they thought they knew who was calling but were simply mistaken.

The same concept also may apply to precognitive dreaming. People often remember fragments of one or more of their dreams the following morning. However, if they later encounter an event that seems to match a dream, they might be especially likely to remember this dream, forget about the vast number of dreams that didn't seem predictive, and so overestimate their ability to dream about the future.

I recently conducted a study to explore whether such selective remembering might lead to an increased frequency of precognitive dreams. We asked volunteers to read several accounts of dreams and descriptions of subsequent events. Half of the time there was a strong correspondence between the dream and the event (for example, '*I dreamt that our whole class was cheering and the following day our teacher let us out of class early*'), while the other half of the time there were much lower levels of correspondence ('*I dreamt that our whole class was cheering and the following day our teacher gave us extra homework*'). Volunteers were then given a surprise memory test and asked to recall as many of the accounts as possible. The results were striking, with volunteers being twice as likely to remember accounts that contained high levels of correspondences.

ASSESSING PRECOGNITIVE DREAMING

I am often contacted by people who claim that their dreams sometimes predict the future. Some of these people are writing to me because they are worried about their experiences; others simply want to participate in research into the phenomena. I often ask people to keep a specially designed dream diary in order to help discover whether their experiences are caused by factors such as selective remembering.

The diary asks them to spend a few moments each morning noting down any dreams that they can remember from the previous night. This helps to prevent them selectively remembering those dreams that correspond to events in the future, or misremembering the dreams to fit those events.

In addition, when they think that one of their dreams has predicted the future, the diary encourages them to note down the predicted event in as much detail as possible, think about any possible hidden causes that might underlie the experience, ask other people for their opinion about the degree of correspondence between the event and the dream, and also take into account the large amount of dreaming going on each night across the world.

People using the diary often re-evaluate their experiences and conclude that there is a normal explanation for their seemingly psychic ability. Others insist that they have an exceptional ability, and these people can be tested using some of the techniques that will be discussed in the next section of this book.

Conclusion

Researchers have investigated many of the psychological mechanisms that cause people to incorrectly believe that they have had a psychic experience. This research has focused on the role played by four key factors: unconscious cognition, the propensity to find correspondences, selective memory, and a poor understanding of probability. Much of the work has demonstrated that these factors do indeed cause people to believe that they have had a psychic experience when, in reality, that is not the case. This work, although vitally important in understanding the psychology of such experiences, does not rule out the possible existence of genuine psychic phenomena. Research into the psychology underlying some psychic experiences has helped mainstream psychologists to understand more about the ways in which people can mislead themselves when they think about their everyday experiences, and helps illustrate why many parapsychologists do not view such experiences as compelling evidence of the paranormal. Seeking to provide such evidence, many parapsychologists have moved into the laboratory in order to test psychic abilities under more controlled conditions.

Section 3
Laboratory research

Telepathy and clairvoyance in the laboratory

From the archive ...

I seem to be able to tell who is on the phone when it is ringing (obviously I don't use caller ID!). I can do this even when the caller is someone completely unexpected, though my abilities are stronger when the caller is someone to whom I am emotionally attached. I reckon on average I'm right about 80% of the time, which is surely far greater than you'd expect by chance. Can you advise how I could conduct a controlled test of this ability?

(Jonathan, aged 36)

Telepathy is the ability to read another person's thoughts (like Jonathan knowing who is calling him before he picks up the telephone handset); and clairvoyance is the ability to detect unknown information (for instance, being able to describe the buildings in a street you've never visited). It's often difficult to be certain that normal means of communication or inference have not contributed to spontaneous instances of telepathy or clairvoyance. For instance, perhaps Jonathan unconsciously anticipates some callers because they ring fairly regularly, or maybe you forgot that you once saw a photograph of the street that you'd never visited. In the laboratory, researchers can devise experiments that rule out some of the issues that make real-world psychic experiences difficult to interpret. Parapsychologists have carried out a large number of laboratory-based studies investigating the possible existence of telepathy and clairvoyance. This work is often highly controversial, with proponents arguing that the findings support the existence of psychic ability, and critics pointing out methodological shortcomings and statistical errors. The renowned methodologist Robert Rosenthal has stated of this debate: 'it has yielded an especially high light/heat ratio'. Let's take a closer look at how laboratory tests of telepathy and clairvoyance have challenged the scientific establishment.

J.B. Rhine: The founding father of parapsychology

Around the turn of the twentieth century, psychologist John Edgar Coover conducted the first university-based ESP experiments in America. Coover's five-year project was carried out at Stanford University, and involved hundreds of volunteers (mainly undergraduates) participating in experiments exploring both telepathy and clairvoyance. In 1917, Coover published a 600-page report describing this work and noting that the results were consistent with chance. Although Coover believed his findings didn't support the existence of ESP, his research did demonstrate that it was possible to scientifically investigate the existence of psychic ability, and encouraged many academics to adopt a more open-minded attitude towards parapsychology. During the 1920s and 1930s, a handful of other researchers conducted additional experiments into psychic ability, but the most influential work was undertaken by Joseph Banks (J.B.) Rhine at Duke University in North Carolina.

In 1927, William McDougall became the head of Duke University's Psychology Department. McDougall was a strong proponent of animism (the belief that all animals, plants, and inanimate objects possess a spiritual essence) and thought that evidence of ESP would help prove the existence of a nonphysical life force. Soon after taking on the role of departmental head, McDougall employed a plant physiologist named J.B. Rhine to conduct ESP research. In the same way that the formation of the Society for Psychical Research is often viewed as the birth of psychical research, so Rhine's appointment at Duke University is usually seen as the beginning of academic parapsychology. Even before he came to Duke, Rhine had impressed McDougall with his determination to take a scientific approach to studying psychic abilities.

Both J.B. Rhine and his wife Louisa became interested in the paranormal in 1922, after hearing a lecture by Sir Arthur Conan Doyle. Doyle was on a tour promoting Spiritualism and psychical research, and particularly championed a famous Boston medium named Mina 'Margery' Crandon. Impressed by Doyle's testimony and distinguished supporters, the Rhines determined to study mediumistic claims scientifically. In 1926, they moved to Boston, a hotbed of psychical research, but were often far from convinced by the séance-room phenomena that they encountered. Indeed, after sitting with Margery, the Rhines concluded that she was a fraud. They wrote imploringly to her sponsors, the American Society for Psychical Research, noting: 'The whole case is sure to crash ... We will be the laughing stock of the world for years to come!' The Rhines went on to write a high-profile exposé of the medium in the *Journal of Abnormal and Social Psychology*, ironically leading Doyle to write in outrage to a Boston newspaper: 'J.B. Rhine is an ass'.

When Rhine arrived at Duke University, he decided to abandon his séance-room investigations and instead focus on laboratory-based ESP research, because it was easier to exert control over experimental conditions in the laboratory. Rhine proved to be both a charismatic and visionary figure, and pioneered a radically new approach to parapsychology.

THE RHINEAN REVOLUTION

Two principal features characterize Rhine's approach to parapsychology.

First, he created a new form of stimuli for ESP testing. In the past, researchers had tended to use playing cards as targets. However, Rhine was worried that some playing cards could be easily confused with one another because they looked similar (such as the six of hearts and the six of diamonds). Rhine invited a perceptual psychologist named Karl Zener to design a series of symbols that would be far more perceptually distinct. Zener came up with five black geometric symbols on a white background: a cross, a circle, three wavy lines, a star, and a square (see Figure 3). Each symbol was printed on a separate card about the size of a playing card, and during Rhine's studies participants were asked to psychically guess the identity of each symbol. The clear-cut nature of the symbols meant that each trial could be unambiguously scored as a 'hit' or a 'miss'.

Second, Rhine focused on the statistical evaluation of experiments by conducting studies using standardized packs of Zener cards. These packs of twenty-five cards contained each of the five symbols repeated five times. During Rhine's studies, participants were asked to psychically determine the order of the cards in a pack, and so would achieve a 20% hit rate (one in five) by chance alone. During a typical study, participants would be asked to guess the order of several packs of cards, often taking part in hundreds or even thousands of trials. Rhine then tabulated the results, counted the number of hits obtained, and calculated the exact statistical outcome of the experiment.

Figure 3 ESP card symbols

Perhaps because of Rhine's negative experience with the medium Margery Crandon, he never invited professional psychics to participate in his experiments. Instead, he began working with staff and students at Duke University, searching for people who appeared able to exhibit and maintain impressive levels of scoring in ESP tests (see Appendix). Rhine eventually focused on just eight participants, with most of the work exploring how their ESP ability was affected by various factors, such as whether the participants in a telepathy study were friends or strangers, or the distance between participants and the Zener cards.

In 1934, Rhine published the methods and results of this research in his first book *Extrasensory Perception*. Rhine argued that the findings from several studies supported the existence of ESP, and that participants' psychic ability systematically varied with several factors. To Rhine, these impressive results suggested that 'ESP is a natural mode of perception and an integral part of mental life.'

'THE WORLD'S FIRST META-ANALYSIS'

To quantify the combined results from a large number of studies, modern-day researchers often employ a statistical technique known as 'meta-analysis'. This technique was first used in medical research in the late 1970s, and in mainstream psychology about a decade later. However, Rhine's research in parapsychology pre-dates this work. In 1940, Rhine and his colleagues examined the combined results of laboratory-based ESP research conducted between 1882 and 1939. This analysis was described in their subsequent book on the topic, *Extrasensory Perception After Sixty Years* (often referred to as 'ESP-60'), and has been described by Freiberg University Hospital epidemiologist Holger Bösch as 'the first comprehensive meta-analysis in the history of science'. Bösch argues that ESP-60 was decades ahead of its time, with Rhine and colleagues developing novel ways of statistically combining data from over a hundred experiments, discussing so-called publication bias (the distortion of conclusions by unpublished studies), and thoroughly evaluating the methodological strengths and weaknesses of each study. In short, ESP-60 was an innovative attempt to draw conclusions from a large and diverse body of research. It was years ahead of similar work in mainstream psychology and medical science, and illustrates Rhine's pioneering approach within parapsychology.

The critics respond

Rhine's monograph sparked a heated controversy, with much of the debate focusing on his statistical methods and experimental controls.

Some of the criticisms were justified. For example, during some of Rhine's telepathy studies, the volunteers playing the roles of 'sender' and 'receiver' were in the same room, allowing the possibility of the receiver inadvertently picking up subtle signals, such as sub-vocal whispering or postural changes, from the sender. In addition, the participants' guesses were manually recorded, and so susceptible to error and bias. Some researchers have attempted to estimate whether error and biased recordings could have distorted Rhine's card-guessing results. A study published in 1939 by Kennedy and Uphoff in the *Journal of Parapsychology* found that psychology students who strongly believed in ESP tended to make about 1% errors when manually recording ESP scores, and 80% of these errors inflated the scores. This research provides only circumstantial evidence that manual recording may have introduced systematic errors into Rhine's results. But, for many, the mere potential for sensory cueing or experimenter error provides a more plausible explanation than extrasensory perception for above-chance performance. Kennedy and Uphoff called for objective methods of scoring to be introduced.

However, other accusations seemed somewhat unreasonable. Take, for example, Charles Hansel's criticisms of Rhine's 'Pearce-Pratt' experiments. In the early 1930s, divinity student Hubert Pearce participated in a number of card-guessing studies conducted by parapsychologist Joseph Gaither Pratt. Pratt and Pearce were located in two separate buildings on the Duke campus. Having synchronized their watches, Pratt would walk to one of the buildings and remove an ESP card from the top of a shuffled deck at predetermined times. Meanwhile, Pearce would be in a separate building and attempt to guess the nature of each card. As this experiment tested the possible existence of clairvoyance, Pratt did not look at the faces of the cards until the end of the session, when he made a written record of the sequence of cards. Pearce's and Pratt's records of target sequences and guesses showed an impressive level of correspondence.

Hansel was alarmed that Pearce had been unsupervised during the study, and wondered whether he could have surreptitiously crossed the campus and secretly observed Pratt preparing his record of the target card sequence. Having visited the Duke campus in the 1960s, Hansel argued that Pearce could have hidden in an empty classroom across the hall from Pratt, and observed him through two glass windows above the doors of the two rooms. However, parapsychologist Ian Stevenson pointed out that Hansel's hypothesis was based on the 1960s layout: 1930s blueprints indicated no direct line of sight from the classroom to Pratt's room. Hansel then modified his hypothesis to suggest that Pearce may have instead peeked directly through the window at the top of Pratt's door. However, this scenario greatly increased the risk of being caught cheating, as Pearce would have needed to stand conspicuously on a chair or a ladder to reach the window.

Over time, Rhine tightened his procedures to deal with the various objections raised by critics. As the controls became tighter, the results of his high-scoring subjects started to decline. Many critics concluded that scoring declined *because* the methods were improved, suggesting that the early high scores were due to methodological weaknesses. However, Rhine attributed the decline in performance to a change in the mindset at this laboratory. Looking back in 1964, he commented that many experimenters adopted a more defensive and critical attitude towards testing, and that this adversely affected results:

> We had in those early years at Duke a very special situation and it was largely responsible for the unusual and unequalled production of results in ESP experiments ... [Following publication of *Extrasensory Perception*] attention concentrated on disputes over experimental precautions, interpretation of results ... and, in the years of tension and contention, the wonderful good fun of the early Duke days was lost and forgotten.

Rhine's declining results caused many parapsychologists gradually to move away from relatively dull and sterile card-guessing procedures, and develop new and more exciting forms of testing (see Appendix).

THE PROBLEM OF FRAUD

Some critics have attempted to undermine laboratory-based evidence for ESP by raising the issue of experimenter fraud. In fact, parapsychology has been shaken by two high-profile scandals in which experimenters have faked their data. The first instance concerned one of Rhine's co-researchers, Walter Levy. Levy had impressed Rhine with his consistently positive results suggestive of psychic capabilities in animals. However, in 1974, some of Levy's colleagues became suspicious and secretly observed him conducting his studies. After just a few days, they caught Levy tampering with his data. Rhine immediately dismissed Levy and declared all of his previous data suspect. The second major case involved British mathematics lecturer Samuel Soal. In the late 1930s, Soal attempted to replicate Rhine's results, and carried out a lengthy and ultimately successful series of ESP studies with a subject named Basil Shackleton. Soal had been a vocal critic of Rhine's findings; therefore, many regarded his work as persuasive evidence for ESP. When criticisms began to emerge about irregularities in Soal's data, several parapsychologists mounted a staunch defence. But doubts persisted until the 1970s, when the painstaking work of British researcher Betty Markwick conclusively demonstrated that Soal had altered his scoring sheets so as to inflate the number of hits in his work with Shackleton. It's worth pointing out that, in this and most other cases of deception in parapsychology, it was the careful scrutiny of parapsychologists themselves, and not external critics, that uncovered malpractice.

Is fraud a problem unique to parapsychology? In 2012, Leslie John of Harvard University Business School administered an anonymous survey of questionable research practices (QRPs) to over two thousand experimental psychologists. Perhaps surprisingly, 0.6% of researchers personally admitted to fraud. When an imaginary 'truth serum' was applied (asking the respondents what they thought *other* researchers were doing), the estimated rate of fraud increased to 1.7%. John concluded that QRPs (of which researcher fraud is just one example) were 'the prevailing norm' in psychology. Dutch parapsychologist Dick Bierman has estimated that rates of fraud in parapsychology are comparable to those in experimental psychology. However, perhaps because parapsychologists are generally more willing to investigate and report fraud, instances of fraud in parapsychology may be more noticeable than in other research areas.

Dream telepathy

During the early 1960s, American psychoanalyst Montague Ullman began to explore the role of dream analysis during therapy.

Ullman found the topic fascinating and eventually helped found the Maimonides Dream Laboratory in New York to explore the science of dreaming. In the late 1960s and early 1970s, Ullman teamed up with parapsychologists Stanley Krippner and Charles Honorton to conduct ten studies exploring the possible existence of dream telepathy.

In a typical Maimonides telepathy experiment, one participant (the 'receiver') arrived at the laboratory towards the start of the evening and had sensors applied to monitor their brainwaves and eye movements. They then climbed into bed and went to sleep. Throughout the night, experimenters observed the volunteer's physiological data. Whenever the participant's eye movements indicated that they were dreaming, the experimenters woke them up and asked them to describe the dream. Meanwhile, a second participant (the 'sender') spent the night in another room at the laboratory, and periodically concentrated on a randomly selected image of a famous painting. After the experimenters had completed a series of trials (seven to twelve nights for each experiment), they ranked the degree of similarity between the image and dream report, with significantly large amounts of similarity being seen as indicative of ESP. Ullman and Krippner described the results of these studies in their book *Dream Telepathy*, arguing that their findings supported the existence of ESP.

In the same way that Rhine's work attracted a considerable amount of critical commentary, so the Maimonides dream studies were subjected to sceptical scrutiny. In 1985, Yale University psychologist Irvin Child reviewed these criticisms. Child noted that some of the scepticism was justified. For example, the Maimonides researchers had developed several ways of assessing the outcome of their experiments; therefore, some critics argued that the experimenters were free to choose whatever analyses gave them a positive result. In contrast,

Child noted that other criticisms seemed less reasonable, and that some sceptics had even grossly misrepresented the experimental procedures used at Maimonides. For example, psychologists Leonard Zusne and Warren Jones wrongly stated that the Maimonides experimenters showed the target picture to the receiver *before* they went to sleep. In fact, in their report describing the studies, the Maimonides researchers had made it clear that they had gone to considerable effort to shield the ESP target from the receiver. Child concluded that the standard of scientific discourse shown by many of the critics was lamentable, and attributed this sloppiness to 'misconception and prejudice'.

In 2013, University of Northampton parapsychologists Simon Sherwood and Chris Roe reviewed nearly half a century of dream-ESP research, comparing the Maimonides findings with the findings of studies conducted after the Maimonides studies. In brief, the impressive results of the early studies were not found in more recent work (for the statistically minded, the effect size r dropped from .33 to .11 with the combined results of the post-Maimonides studies being barely significant). Researchers disagree about the reason for this lack of replication. Sceptics argued that the Maimonides results may have been spurious because they contained methodological and statistical weaknesses, as noted by Child. In contrast, ESP proponents noted that the Maimonides studies were conducted in a sleep laboratory that enabled researchers to monitor and awaken participants after each dream. Dream reports obtained in this way would be less susceptible to faulty recollection than reports gathered upon awakening in the morning. Proponents have also noted that many of the Maimonides studies used specially selected subjects (see box), whereas the more recent studies tended to involve participants who didn't claim any special psychic abilities.

DREAM TELEPATHY AND THE GRATEFUL DEAD

In 1971, the rock group the Grateful Dead held a series of six concerts at the Capitol Theatre in New York. These concerts formed the basis for one of the most unusual experiments in the history of parapsychology. The band members were curious about ESP and had previously visited Stanley Krippner at the Maimonides Dream Laboratory. Krippner developed a strong friendship with the band, sometimes hypnotizing the drummers Mickey Hart and Bill Kreutzmann so that they could perfectly synchronize their playing. Jerry Garcia suggested that the band team up with the laboratory and conduct a mass experiment into dream telepathy. Krippner agreed, and on each night of the Capitol Theatre concerts their two-thousand-strong audience acted as senders in a dream telepathy study. The experienced dream telepathy subject Malcolm Bessent acted as receiver, sleeping at the Maimonides Dream Laboratory some forty-five miles from the concert.

Ullman and Krippner noted that 'the majority of the audience were already in altered states of consciousness by target time'. At 11.30pm, the fans were shown a slide stating: 'Try using your ESP to "send" this picture to Malcolm Bessent. He will try to dream about the picture ...' The randomly selected target picture was then projected onto a large screen while the Grateful Dead continued to rock and roll. Bessent was awoken throughout the night and asked to describe his dreams.

Bessent scored significantly above chance, and the study illustrates how parapsychologists can conduct innovative research outside of the laboratory. Having published an academic paper on the project, Krippner is acknowledged as the 'godfather' of the Grateful Dead Scholar's Caucus.

Altered states of consciousness

Many parapsychologists were eager to build on the success of the Maimonides dream studies, but reluctant to spend night after night running experiments. As a result, they started to develop new ways of exploring the relationship between altered states of consciousness and psychic functioning, with much of this work centring on a mild sensory isolation technique called the 'ganzfeld' procedure.

The ganzfeld (German for 'entire field') procedure was originally developed by perceptual psychologists to explore the effects of minimizing sensory input, and introduced to parapsychology in the mid-1970s by Charles Honorton and William Braud. Honorton and Braud hypothesized that the procedure might help boost ESP performance by removing other sources of sensory distraction.

In a typical ganzfeld ESP study, one volunteer (the 'receiver') is placed into mild sensory isolation. They are asked to sit in a comfortable reclining chair in a sound-insulated room, wear headphones and translucent goggles, and are bathed in red light. After hearing a short relaxation exercise, white noise (a sound like radio static) is played over the receiver's headphones, and they then spend around twenty minutes describing the thoughts and images that flow through their mind. In a separate room, another participant (the 'sender') looks at a randomly chosen target (such as an art print or photograph) and attempts to psychically send it to the receiver. Later, the receiver is shown four possible targets (the actual target and three decoys) and is asked to identify the image that most resembles their thoughts and images. A ganzfeld experiment involves a large number of such trials, with each trial usually involving a different pair of participants.

When the results of these trials are combined, participants would be expected to choose the correct target 25% of the time by chance alone. Significant scoring above this level is seen as evidence of ESP. In addition to looking at the overall hit rate of studies, parapsychologists have explored the impact of several factors, including, for example, using film clips as targets and highly creative individuals as participants.

The ganzfeld debate

In 1978, Honorton collected together the results from forty-two ganzfeld experiments that had been conducted in nine different laboratories. He discovered that 55% of the studies had obtained positive results, whereas only 5% would have been expected by chance. In the same way that the positive results from both Rhine's ESP work and the Maimonides dream-telepathy studies generated a considerable amount of debate, so Honorton's analysis soon attracted the attention of sceptics. At the forefront of this debate was one of parapsychology's best-informed critics, University of Oregon psychologist Ray Hyman. Between 1983 and 1985, Honorton and Hyman exchanged a series of detailed claims and rebuttals about the studies. Hyman argued that several factors could have inflated the success rate of the experiment, including the selective publication of studies with positive results, multiple ways of measuring the success of studies, sensory leakage between senders and receivers, and poor randomization during the selection of the target.

Honorton countered by meta-analysing a subset of the ganzfeld studies that were less susceptible to these accusations. He reported a highly significant hit rate of 35%, and cautiously concluded that this was a 'step towards replicability'. Hyman agreed that there *was* above-chance scoring in these ganzfeld studies, but continued to maintain that they were far from perfect. Honorton argued against Hyman's criticisms but conceded that the database contained some weaknesses. The exchanges between Hyman and Honorton were often lengthy and detailed, resulting in parapsychologist John Palmer describing them as 'one of the most sophisticated critical exchanges in the history of parapsychology'.

Hyman and Honorton then happened to dine together at the 1986 convention of the Parapsychological Association, and discussed how best to move forward with the debate. In December 1986, they published a 'joint communiqué' in the *Journal of Parapsychology*. This paper set out an agenda for future ganzfeld studies and provided methodological guidelines to address the various weaknesses identified during their exchange. These recommendations contained a range of measures, including preventing sensory leakage between the sender and receiver, developing better randomization methods, and reporting studies regardless of outcome.

The autoganzfeld

By the early 1980s, Honorton was appointed Director of the Psychophysical Research Laboratories (PRL) in New Jersey, and decided to conduct a series of ganzfeld studies that conformed to the guidelines developed in collaboration with Hyman. Honorton designed and built the 'autoganzfeld' – a computer-controlled system that automated many aspects of data collection and analysis. Between 1983 and 1989, Honorton used the system to conduct eleven studies. Together, these studies involved 240 participants, 354 trials, and 8 different experimenters. The studies achieved an overall hit rate of 32%, and Honorton again argued that the data supported the existence of ESP.

In 1991, the PRL closed due to a loss of funding, and Honorton moved to University of Edinburgh's Koestler Parapsychology Unit. There he collaborated with Cornell University social psychologist Daryl Bem on a meta-analysis of the PRL autoganzfeld studies. Sadly, Honorton suffered from congenital health problems, and he died aged forty-six in 1992, only nine days before the meta-analysis was accepted for publication in the leading psychology journal *Psychological Bulletin*.

Bem and Honorton's paper claimed that the results of their

meta-analysis provided 'replicable evidence for an anomalous process of information transfer', and urged other researchers to try to replicate the effect.

Following Bem and Honorton's landmark paper, *Psychological Bulletin* published two further ganzfeld ESP meta-analyses. In 1999, parapsychologists Julie Milton and Richard Wiseman argued that their meta-analysis of studies between 1987 and 1997 demonstrated a 'lack of replication' of Bem and Honorton's findings. Then in 2010, Lance Storm, Patrizio Tressoldi, and Lorenzo di Risio, who analysed studies published between 1997 and 2008, argued that the studies supported the ESP hypothesis, and concluded that 'ganzfeld is one of the most consistent and reliable paradigms in parapsychology'. In each case, considerable debate ensued over how to interpret the outcome of the meta-analysis, with the latest critique appearing in *Psychological Bulletin* in 2013. That these later ganzfeld meta-analyses appeared in one of psychology's leading journals perhaps indicates that parapsychologists are becoming more sophisticated at making their work relevant and acceptable to a mainstream and predominantly sceptical scientific audience.

Some parapsychologists are clearly impressed with the results of the ganzfeld studies and some, such as Professor Chris Roe at the University of Northampton, have determined that they will continue with this line of work. However, others conclude that the time-consuming procedure is inefficient, and may seem rather bizarre to mainstream scientists. As we will see shortly, Daryl Bem has suggested that parapsychologists follow cognitive social psychologists, who are increasingly moving towards the study of unconscious processes employing subtle measures such as participants' performance on reaction-time and memory tasks, rather than asking them to try to make direct verbal reports on their thoughts, feelings, and mental imagery.

THE STRENGTHS AND WEAKNESSES OF META-ANALYSIS

The ganzfeld debate highlights both the strengths and weaknesses of meta-analysis. Meta-analysis is an invaluable tool for identifying patterns in the results of a large number of studies, and these discoveries can generate hypotheses for future research. However, when a meta-analysis is designed and conducted *after* individual studies have been carried out (which is the norm), it cannot provide clear-cut evidence about the existence or non-existence of ESP. There are several different ways in which researcher bias can influence the outcome of a meta-analysis. Take, for example, the decision about which studies to include. If researchers know the outcome of some individual studies, then this process can be deliberately or inadvertently biased. For example, if researchers know that ganzfeld studies using film clips as targets have obtained relatively high hit rates, then they might decide to focus on this subset of studies, thereby creating a meta-analysis that was very likely to have a highly positive outcome. To avoid this type of bias, researchers should outline the criteria for the individual studies they will include *prior* to these studies being conducted. The same goes for other decisions about how the meta-analysis will be conducted. Unfortunately, this type of meta-analysis of ganzfeld studies has not been conducted to date. (Parapsychologists are no different to academic psychologists in this respect; this kind of 'prospective' meta-analysis is rarely conducted outside of medical research.) To support this effort, the Koestler Parapsychology Unit runs a study registry (see *Further reading* for a link) where researchers can pre-register both individual studies and meta-analyses prior to undertaking the work. It is hoped that this initiative will help resolve the ESP debate.

Conclusion

Parapsychologists have developed several different methods for researching the possible existence of telepathy and clairvoyance. In Rhine's early work, this involved participants attempting to guess the identity of Zener cards. At Maimonides Dream Laboratory researchers explored whether the dream state was associated with psychic functioning. Finally, in the ganzfeld procedure, participants are placed in a situation where sensory distractions are minimized and are asked to describe a remote target. The researchers carrying out these studies have claimed that the results of the work support the existence of ESP. Some of these claims have been published in leading mainstream psychology journals, indicating that the work is judged to have met high scientific standards. Despite this, some sceptics have argued that these studies contain methodological and statistical shortcomings. Although not all of this criticism has been deserved, overall the field has benefited from such scrutiny because it has led to a range of methodological improvements, including those designed to minimize publication bias, sensory leakage, and poor randomization. Indeed, such improvements may be one of the greatest benefits to come out of the work. As Harvard University social psychologist Robert Rosenthal stated: 'Science in general and parapsychological inquiry in particular have been well served by the recent ganzfeld debate.'

Precognition in the laboratory

From the archive ...

I once had a rather strange dream about a broken bottle under the wheel of a car parked by the pavement. At the time the dream seemed very vivid and I couldn't think of any obvious reason why I might be dreaming about such a thing. I forgot all about it until I was walking home from work the next day and noticed a broken bottle poised below a car's wheel. This immediately brought my dream back to mind. Was this just an odd coincidence? Did my dream make me pay more attention than usual to the wheels of parked cars, or did it somehow predict the future?

(Simon, aged 24)

Surveys suggest that about 25% of people believe that they have had a precognitive experience. Parapsychologists have developed a range of experimental techniques to investigate such experiences, including collating passenger numbers on ill-fated trains, asking people to predict the sequence of randomly illuminating lights, monitoring dreams, and measuring whether volunteers become especially anxious before receiving an unexpected electric shock.

Precognition in everyday life

We have already learned how Joseph Banks Rhine joined Duke University in the late 1920s and began to scientifically study the possible existence of ESP. This work was widely reported in the media, resulting in Rhine frequently receiving anecdotal accounts of paranormal experiences from members of the public. In the late 1940s, Rhine's wife, Louisa Rhine, started to collect and collate these reports. Over time, Louisa Rhine amassed over ten thousand cases and her database remains the most extensive collection in existence. The vast majority of experiences in Louisa Rhine's database relate to precognition, with around half of these involving dreaming. For example, one woman reported a precognitive dream experience that took place when she was seven years old. One day, her housemaid sent her out into the garden to play. She eventually fell asleep in the garden and dreamed about her mother walking away from her down an avenue of trees. During the dream, she ran as fast as she could after her mother, but simply couldn't catch up with her. Her mother then turned around and said, 'Go back, my daughter, your father needs you.' The girl suddenly awoke from the dream, went back into her house, and met her father in the hallway. Her father hugged her and said, 'Daughter, I need you. Your mother has just left us.' How do parapsychologists assess such experiences?

Researching precognition in everyday life

A small number of researchers have carried out non-laboratory-based studies into the possible existence of precognition. In the 1930s, for example, psychical researcher Theodore Besterman asked a group of volunteers to write an account of their dreams the moment they woke up, and then post these accounts to him prior to their talking to other people, reading a newspaper, or listening to the radio. The volunteers were also asked to send Besterman an account of any subsequent event that seemed to match their dream. Besterman hoped that this technique

would minimize some of the problems associated with anecdotal reports of precognitive experiences including, for example,
the misremembering of dreams and difficulties in assessing the
role of coincidence. Besterman received 430 dream reports and
45 confirming events. However, when he assessed the degree
to which dreams resembled the events, Besterman found only
two instances suggesting a 'good case' for precognition, and
concluded that the study had failed to yield positive results. Over
the years, other researchers have followed in Besterman's footsteps and invited the public to submit their dreams to 'precognition bureaux'. None of these studies have yielded compelling
evidence of precognition.

In the 1950s, parapsychologist William Cox adopted a
completely different approach to assessing precognition. Cox
reasoned that if people could see into the future they might
experience a psychic 'warning' before trips that were going to
involve an accident, and so be more likely to alter or cancel
their travel plans. To test his theory, Cox examined train
records to discover whether passenger numbers were lower
on trains involved in accidents than on the same route in the
weeks before the accident. Despite having access to only a relatively small amount of data, Cox demonstrated a significant
reduction of passenger numbers on trains involved in accidents.
Although Cox's approach was highly innovative, other parapsychologists have pointed out that bad weather might have
both diminished passenger numbers and increased the likelihood of an accident.

The work of Besterman and Cox illustrates the challenges
of trying to test for the existence of precognition in everyday
life. Furthermore, many anecdotal accounts of apparent precognition may have a perfectly normal explanation. For example, a
dream may be misremembered, or the entire experience could
have simply been a coincidence, as people tend to have five or
six dreams every night. Most researchers therefore don't regard

anecdotal accounts as yielding convincing evidence of precognition, but instead use them as a source of naturalistic observations to help guide more controlled research. Indeed, the vast majority of research into precognition has taken place within the controlled confines of the laboratory.

Early experimental work

Much of the early experimental work into precognition was carried out by J.B. Rhine at Duke University in the 1930s, and involved reversing procedures that had been developed to test for clairvoyance. During a typical clairvoyance study, researchers would shuffle decks of Zener cards and then ask volunteers to try to guess the order of the decks. To test for precognition, this procedure was reversed, with volunteers being asked to guess the order of the decks prior to their being shuffled by the researchers. Many of Rhine's initial precognition studies obtained highly positive results. For example, one experiment involved a divinity student named Hubert Pearce. Pearce took part in several large studies in which he attempted to predict the orders of hundreds of decks of Zener cards. As noted in the previous chapter, each deck contained twenty-five cards (five geometrical symbols repeated five times) and so, just by chance, Pearce would have correctly guessed the identity of five cards in each deck. In one study, Pearce correctly guessed an average of 6.3 cards per deck, and in a second experiment he averaged 7.1 cards per deck. Both scores were highly statistically significant.

When Rhine published the results of his studies, sceptics argued that the experiments suffered from various methodological and statistical flaws. For example, some suggested that the Zener cards had not been properly shuffled, meaning that biases in subjects' guesses might have occasionally coincided with biases in the card sequence, inflating the hit rate. Parapsychologists countered this criticism by arguing that the later studies used random number tables rather than hand shuffling to ensure properly random sequences. Precognition studies are also easier to control than telepathy or clairvoyance studies. The precognitive target is not selected until after the subject has made his or her guesses, thus eliminating the possibility of sensory leakage of target information at the time the guesses are made. However, as with Rhine's research into telepathy and clairvoyance, the results of his precognition studies declined over time, and researchers started to move away from card guessing to explore other types of experimental procedures.

In the late 1960s, physicist Helmut Schmidt was working as a senior research scientist at Boeing Scientific Research Laboratories in Seattle. Schmidt had always been interested in parapsychology and eventually convinced his employers to support an experiment into the possible existence of precognition. The resulting study involved a book-sized device that contained four buttons below four coloured lamps. Volunteers were asked to guess which lamp would light up in a few moments' time, and then press the button below that lamp. This button press triggered a random number generator (RNG) in the device and this, in turn, selected and illuminated one of the four lamps. Schmidt arranged for three volunteers to make a total of 63,066 guesses. By chance, they should have correctly predicted which lamp was about to illuminate 25% of the time. In fact, they were right just over 26% of the time, which, given the large number of trials involved, was highly statistically significant.

As is often the case with parapsychology experiments that obtain positive results, Schmidt's work was subject to considerable criticism. For example, psychologist Ray Hyman from the University of Oregon suggested that the selection of the lights in Schmidt's studies was not truly random. To counter this criticism, Schmidt programmed the RNG to carry out a series of five million dummy trials, and demonstrated that the choice of

lamp was indeed random. Hyman argued that this did not duplicate the typical conditions of an actual experimental session, and
Schmidt responded by testing the RNG under much more realistic conditions and again showed that the choice of lamp was
adequately random.

Schmidt's work demonstrated that asking volunteers to try
to predict the output of an RNG was an efficient and effective way of testing for precognition. Because of this, many other
parapsychologists developed similar types of RNG-precognition
experiments. In 1989, Charles Honorton and Diane Ferrari of
the Psychophysical Research Laboratories carried out a meta-
analysis of precognition experiments that had been conducted
between 1935 and 1987. They analysed the results from over
three hundred studies reported by more than sixty researchers. Overall, the results were highly statistically significant,
thus supporting the precognition hypothesis. However, some
researchers have raised concerns about the meta-analysis, noting
that it combined experiments that had employed quite different
methods (such as Rhine's Zener card tests and Schmidt's automated lamp studies), and that the results from these studies were
quite different from one another. Such diversity is problematic,
in part, because it suggests that the studies are examining quite
different phenomena and so shouldn't be combined into a single
analysis.

DREAM PRECOGNITION

The team that conducted the dream telepathy research conducted
at the Maimonides Dream Laboratory in New York during the
1960s and 1970s also ran two dream precognition studies with the
gifted participant Malcolm Bessent. In each experiment, Bessent
was invited to dream about the type of images and sounds that
he would see and hear the following morning. The next day,

the researchers randomly selected a picture and soundtrack, and played it to Bessent. The studies yielded highly positive results. In 2013, I teamed up with researchers Laurène Vuillaume and Richard Wiseman, and attempted to replicate these studies. Twenty volunteers who claimed to have previously experienced precognitive dreams spent a night at the Edinburgh Sleep Centre. Throughout the night, they were woken up and asked to report their dreams. The following morning, they were shown a randomly chosen film clip, and an independent judge then compared the content of the dream with the film clip. The results did not support the existence of precognition. When I present this study at conferences, I ask the audience why they think our results were different to those obtained during the original Maimonides work. Proponents of precognition often point out that our volunteers may not have been as psychically gifted as the Maimonides special subject Malcolm Bessent. In contrast, sceptics argue that the original studies may have been methodologically flawed, and that our study failed to find an effect because precognition doesn't exist. It is a compelling illustration of how people's beliefs affect the way in which they interpret the outcome of research.

From precognition to presentiment

Much of the laboratory-based research into the possible existence of precognition has involved asking volunteers to attempt to consciously predict the future (the word 'cognition' denoting a conscious thought). However, some researchers have argued that it might be better to move away from conscious guessing and instead focus on exploring volunteers' hunches, intuitions, and 'gut feelings'. Various phrases, such as 'feeling the future', have been used for this latter category of research, but the word 'presentiment' perhaps expresses the concept most concisely.

Psychologist Rex Stanford from St John's University in New York has developed one of the best-known theories associated with this approach, known as 'Psi-Mediated Instrumental

Response' (PMIR). Stanford speculated that precognition may have evolved because it helps organisms to unconsciously avoid future danger.

Stanford offers the following incident as an illustration of how his theory might operate. He is a keen birdwatcher and, driving home one night, he suddenly had an impulse to detour past a nearby lake to view its birdlife. It was only when he arrived at the lake that he realized it made no sense to have taken the detour because it was dark. Stanford couldn't even see the lake, never mind the birds. Later, he learned of a serious road traffic accident on his normal route home. So, according to the PMIR theory, Stanford may have unconsciously seen into the future and avoided the dangers associated with the accident.

Stanford's model predicts that instances of precognition will often occur in the form of fortuitous coincidences or gut feelings. Some of the research in this area has involved examining whether people feel especially anxious when they are about to experience some type of negative event. When a person is relaxed their skin is relatively dry, but when they become anxious they start to sweat. These variations in moisture levels result in changes to the skin's electrical conductivity or, as psychophysiologists refer to it, electrodermal activity (EDA). In the 1960s, Hungarian parapsychologist Zoltan Vassy carried out a precognition study in which he continuously measured people's EDA while they received randomly timed electric shocks. In his original studies, the volunteers did indeed become more anxious moments before the shock, but these positive findings disappeared when Vassy improved the methodology of the study.

In the mid-1990s, Vassy's novel approach to precognition caught the attention of parapsychologists Dean Radin from the Institute of Noetic Sciences and Dick Bierman from the University of Amsterdam. Radin and Bierman decided to compare volunteers' EDA immediately before they were shown either a shocking photograph or a more neutral one. Radin and Bierman found that their volunteers were indeed especially anxious just prior to seeing the shocking photograph, and argued that their results supported the existence of precognition.

As is often the case with new research methods, Radin and Bierman's initial studies contained some potential methodological issues. For example, Swedish psychologist Jan Dalkvist noted that, if the volunteers had not seen a shocking photograph for some time during the study, their arousal might gradually increase in anticipation, and therefore be especially high when such a photograph is eventually displayed to them. Radin conceded that this was theoretically possible, but re-analysed his data and demonstrated that this potential problem wasn't responsible for his positive findings.

Feeling the future

Cornell University psychologist Daryl Bem has recently introduced a new method for testing precognition. Like much of the previous work in the field, this technique avoids the need for volunteers to engage in any form of conscious guessing. In addition, unlike the ganzfeld procedure discussed earlier, or studies involving the measuring of volunteers' physiology, Bem's technique is easy to carry out, doesn't require any specialist equipment, and is based on a well-established finding from cognitive psychology.

Psychologists have long conducted studies in which they have shown participants a list of words and asked them to mentally repeat certain words on the list (this is known as 'rehearsal'). The participants are then asked to remember the words and, unsurprisingly, the words that they mentally rehearsed are more likely to be recalled. Bem flipped this idea around, and examined whether rehearsed words would be more easily remembered when the memory test occurs *before* the rehearsal.

During a typical Bem study, volunteers sit in front of a computer and are asked to remember the list of words that are presented on the computer screen. They are then given a memory test and asked to write down all of the words that they can remember from the list. After the test, the computer randomly selects half of the words from the original list and shows them again to the participants. Bem expected to find a kind of precognitive memory effect, predicting that during the memory test the volunteers would be especially likely to remember more of the words they were *about* to see.

In 2011, Bem published a paper describing nine experiments using this general technique. All but one of the studies obtained a statistically significant result. Bem's paper was published in a mainstream psychology journal (the *Journal of Personality and Social Psychology*), and generated a great deal of discussion within parapsychology, psychology, and the media. For example, psychologists Jeffrey Rouder (University of Missouri) and Richard Morey (University of Groningen) published a meta-analysis of Bem's studies using what they felt was a more appropriate statistical method (known as a Bayes factor analysis). They concluded that Bem's findings were 'worthy of notice' but did not provide viable evidence for ESP due to the lack of a convincing mechanism for this alleged psychic ability. This illustrates the challenge that parapsychologists face in gaining wider acceptance of claimed positive findings.

Because Bem's studies employed adaptations of regular psychology experiments, several other psychologists have suggested that his positive findings are symptomatic of systemic problems with how psychologists conduct their studies and analyse their data – an issue that we'll expand upon in this book's conclusion. To his credit, Bem encouraged other researchers to try to replicate his experiments, and made his computer program and other necessary materials publicly available. Some research-ers have since reported results consistent with the precognition hypothesis, while others have failed to find any evidence to support the existence of precognition.

When an experiment is simple to conduct, it can be simple to discard. Due to the ease of conducting these 'feeling the future' experiments, there is a risk of publication bias (failing to report studies that did not confirm the experimenter's expectations). So, study registration will be important to remove the risk of publication bias in this emerging area of research. Usually publi-cation bias in parapsychology is framed as psi proponents failing to report studies that obtain chance results. Note, however, that publication bias can cut both ways. A sceptical researcher may be reluctant to publish a study that obtains support for precognition and it is not difficult to imagine how a mainstream researcher might find themselves in this position. Currently, a large-scale multi-centre pre-registered project is being coordinated by para-psychologists at the Institute of Noetic Sciences (IONS) and Bem himself. It is too soon to judge the overall picture emerging from these experiments, and only time will tell whether Bem's technique will provide compelling evidence of precognition.

Conclusion

Parapsychologists have developed three types of experimental techniques to investigate the possible existence of precognition. First, some of the work has looked at the phenomenon in every-day life, and involved setting up 'precognition bureaux' and monitoring passenger numbers on trains that were subsequently involved in accidents. Second, other work has been laboratory based, and involved asking participants to predict the identity of shuffled decks of Zener cards and the output of random number generators. A third and final strand of work has focused on volunteers' unconscious reactions, including their physiology and performance on memory tests. Many of these studies have yielded positive results and some parapsychologists believe that they provide strong evidence in favour of precognition. However, others are less certain, and some sceptics have criticized the methodology and statistical procedures employed in some of the experiments. As is so often the case with experimental parapsychology, there is no real consensus about the results of this work. What is clear, however, is that, as experimental methods have gradually become more rigorous, results supporting the precognition hypothesis have become more difficult for critics to casually dismiss.

11

Mental influence in the laboratory: Physical and biological

From the archive ...

I twisted my back a few months ago. It was really painful, but aside from prescribing painkillers my GP wasn't able to help at all. Eventually I was so desperate I asked my friends for help, and one of them recommended a Reiki healer who would come to my house (I could barely walk down the street). I always thought Reiki was mumbo jumbo, but when this lady placed her palms on my back, I felt an immense heat and tingling radiating out from her hands. Afterwards, I definitely felt less pain, and the next day I could walk much better.

(Brad, aged 56)

Earlier, we saw how researchers have investigated the mind-over-matter feats of claimants such as Uri Geller, James Hydrick, and Ted Serios. Often, it is difficult to rule out the possibility of sleight-of-hand in these cases, particularly when dealing with charismatic and idiosyncratic personalities who frustrate the researchers' attempts to instigate proper controls. Most parapsychologists examining psychokinesis now tend to avoid these potentially problematic types of investigations, and instead focus on two other strands of research. The first strand examines 'micro-PK' – the influence of the mind on random physical systems, such as the roll of dice and random number generators. The second strand examines whether the mind can influence biological systems, including, for example, the growth of plant seeds and people's physiological activity and well-being. By looking at how the mind may influence these delicate physical systems, parapsychologists are pushing at the boundaries of established sciences such as physics.

Physical systems

The pioneering work of J.B. Rhine in the late 1920s helped establish parapsychology as an academic discipline. Rhine's initial work focused on the scientific investigation of ESP. However, in 1934, Rhine received a visit from a professional gambler who claimed that he could mentally affect the outcome of dice rolls in a casino. Intrigued, Rhine decided to conduct a series of studies in which volunteers were asked to use their psychic abilities to influence the roll of dice (see Appendix).

By the start of the 1940s, Rhine and his team had completed several large-scale dice studies, and the combined results from over 600,000 trials were highly statistically significant. Unfortunately, much of this work was poorly controlled. For example, many of the dice throws were made by hand and may not have been truly random, and the results of the studies were frequently manually recorded and therefore open to error. Over the years, researchers working with Rhine attempted to eliminate these problems. For example, in the early 1940s, parapsychologists Edmond and Lottie Gibson replaced hand rolling with a rotating, motor-driven cage that automatically tossed the dice. This system was used to carry out over thirty thousand trials, and again the results were statistically significant.

Many parapsychologists followed in Rhine's footsteps and dice-throwing experiments flourished throughout the 1940s and 1950s. In the 1960s, these studies were critiqued by psychologist Edward Girden from Brooklyn College. Girden mostly attributed the positive results to failures to control for biased dice-throws and errors in statistical analyses. In the 1990s parapsychologist Dean Radin conducted a meta-analysis of the dice-throwing work, collecting together research papers from fifty-two investigators and over two million trials. Radin conceded that the database was far from perfect, but argued that there was a small and statistically significant overall effect that couldn't be attributed to poor methodology.

CASCADING BALLS

One of the more unusual micro-PK set-ups involved the 'random mechanical cascade' devised by engineering professor Robert Jahn at Princeton University. This large device involved an array of pins attached to a vertical wall and encased in glass. To operate the cascade, hundreds of small metal ball-bearings were dropped into a chute at the top of the array. As the balls fell down, they bounced unpredictably on the pins and eventually stacked up at the bottom of the device. The placement of the pins ensured that the balls created a Gaussian distribution (a bell-shaped curve), with most of them falling into the middle of the array and a smaller number ending up on the right and left sides. During Jahn's experiments, volunteers were asked to try to use their psychic abilities to shift the balls to either the right-hand or left-hand side of the distribution. Electronic counters recorded the resulting distributions. Jahn believes that the results from the experiment support the existence of micro-PK.

Random number generators

During the 1960s, parapsychologists eventually lost interest in conducting rather laborious dice studies, and started to work with other types of statistical systems. In so doing, they sought to speed up testing and eliminate experimental error by administering and scoring tests electronically. Earlier, we saw how, in the late 1960s, physicist Helmut Schmidt used random number generators (RNGs) to test for precognition. Schmidt's work involved building a machine that lit up four coloured lamps in an unpredictable order, and asking volunteers to identify which lamp would illuminate next. Schmidt's machine could also be used to test for micro-PK by simply asking volunteers to try to make their chosen lamp light. Although the two studies sound similar, if successful they would produce different patterns of data. In the precognition study, the output from the RNG should be random; however, in the micro-PK study, the RNG output should be biased because it has been influenced by the volunteers' choices. Because all RNG research involves testing micro-PK, it tends just to be called 'PK-RNG' research.

Schmidt ran several PK-RNG studies and reported positive results. Several other parapsychologists, including engineering professor Robert Jahn from Princeton University, followed up on this work and conducted their own PK-RNG studies. In 2006, Holger Bösch (University Hospital Freiburg), Fiona Steinkamp (University of Edinburgh), and Emil Boller (Freiburg Institute for Border Areas of Psychology and Mental Hygiene) carried out a meta-analysis of hundreds of PK-RNG studies and published their findings in a well-known psychology journal, *Psychological Bulletin*.

The studies involved in the meta-analysis were conducted by almost sixty researchers from over thirty institutions, and the methodological quality of the studies was high, with 42% of the studies receiving the highest possible rating.

Overall, the combined results from the studies revealed an extremely small, but statistically significant, effect. The authors wondered whether this small effect might be due to an unusual kind of publication bias. According to their theory, small-scale

PK-RNG studies (that is, studies involving a small number of trials) are relatively easy to conduct and therefore might be likely to remain unpublished if they don't yield evidence of psychic ability. In contrast, larger-scale experiments are more expensive and time-consuming, and are therefore more likely to be reported regardless of their outcome. When Bösch and his co-authors examined the database, they noticed that the largest effects tended to come from the smallest studies. Because of this pattern, the authors suggested that the PK-RNG database may be affected by a publication bias, and so didn't necessarily support the existence of micro-PK. Dean Radin, of the Institute of Noetic Sciences, argued against this idea noting, for example, that it seems unlikely that researchers could have carried out the large number of small-scale studies needed to nullify the reported effects.

Bösch, Steinkamp, and Boller recommended that researchers resolve the issue by carrying out a set of pre-registered PK-RNG studies. In the late-1990s, three parapsychology laboratories did exactly that. They attempted to replicate a set of PK-RNG experiments that had previously obtained significant results. Each laboratory used identical equipment and procedures. The results, reported in 2000, did not support the existence of micro-PK. While some of the researchers involved in micro-PK research were understandably disappointed by the outcome of this collaboration, this ambitious project is a rare example of the kind of coordinated effort needed if parapsychology is to start to provide a definitive answer about the existence of psychic ability.

Precisely *how* could the mind interact with the physical world?

Many parapsychologists focus on trying to demonstrate some kind of inexplicable effect rather than creating a theory that might explain psychic functioning. For example, in ganzfeld ESP studies, the researcher is simply testing whether the participant can correctly identify the ESP target more often than would be expected by chance. If the participant can achieve above-chance scoring, this may be evidence in support of ESP, but it reveals little about how ESP may work. However, other researchers have taken a more theory-based route, arguing that it will be easier to demonstrate psychic effects once one understands how they operate. Much of the recent work in this area has focused on trying to produce a theory that bonds psychic ability, micro-PK, and quantum mechanics (QM; a branch of physics). This is because PK-RNG studies typically ask participants to attempt to influence random number generators whose output derives from unpredictable quantum processes, leading researchers to ponder exactly how the mind might interact with these processes. To explain the theoretical basis for this approach, we will take a short diversion into QM. However, if you are not technically minded, you may skip the next paragraph without missing too much!

Quantum mechanics postulates that extremely small-scale objects, such as sub-atomic particles, behave differently when observed than when unobserved. Until they are observed, such particles are in an indeterminate or 'blurred' state, with the combination of these states being described mathematically by a 'wave function'. But at the moment of observation the inde-terminacy is resolved, corresponding to the so-called 'collapse of the wave function'. A related phenomenon involves the 'entan-glement' of two particles that are physically separated. Until they are observed, both particles are in an indeterminate state, but, when one particle is observed, the indeterminacy of both particles is resolved. Because the measurement of the state of the first particle instantaneously determines the state of the second particle, this process is incompatible with traditional causality so this is more accurately described as a 'non-local correlation' than as an 'influence' of observation over the particles.

So, according to QM, at extremely small scales, the very act of observation or measurement appears to 'influence' the physical system that is being observed. The apparent effect of observation on very small-scale matter has forced physicists to consider the meaning of observation and measurement. Various solutions have been proposed, with a minority of physicists arguing that it is consciousness itself that somehow interacts with these sub-atomic particles. Seen in this way, mind is directly interacting with the physical world, so perhaps it's not surprising that this interpretation of QM captured the attention of some parapsychologists.

In the 1970s, parapsychologists Helmut Schmidt and Evan Harris Walker attempted to link formally this interpretation of QM with psychic phenomena by developing a model of psychic ability known as observational theory. Their model proposed a mechanism whereby an observer can influence the behaviour of the system in the direction of the observer's intention. So, they purport to explain how the participant in PK-RNG studies can alter the output of the random number generator. The theory is highly controversial with, for example, parapsychologist Joop Houtkooper arguing that QM cannot provide a specific mechanism that observational theorists might adapt for their purposes.

Recently, one research team has attempted to resolve the issue by examining the possible effect of conscious observation on a quantum-scale physical system. One of the classic demonstrations in quantum physics involves directing a laser light towards a sheet of metal with two tiny slits. The results demonstrate that light acts both as a wave and a particle. Evidence for its wave-like nature comes from the resulting 'interference pattern' (stripes of regularly varying brightness), and evidence for its particle-like nature comes from data showing that the light travels through the slits one photon at a time. In 2012, Dean Radin and his colleagues published a paper in the journal *Physics Essays* describing six experiments in which volunteers were asked to either direct their attention towards a double-slit optical apparatus or away from it. A further series of control sessions were conducted in which nobody was even present in the room with the apparatus. Radin predicted that the interference pattern would be reduced when the volunteers directed their attention towards the apparatus. The results revealed a highly significant effect. No such effects were observed in the control sessions. The effect also co-varied with several psychological factors (such as whether the participants were meditators), but not with any physical variables (such as the temperature in the room). Similar findings were reported in three follow-up studies reported by Radin and colleagues in the same journal a year later.

By using the double-slit paradigm, Radin is attempting to open physicists' minds to the possibility of psychic ability. However, Radin is cautious about whether these findings should be interpreted in terms of QM. He both encourages independent replication attempts and invites physicists to join in theoretical discussions. Many physicists who are interested in psi feel that QM is relevant but alone cannot provide the full explanation. Others argue that the brain is a relatively large and 'wet' biological object, and that the physical laws governing such systems are quite different to the quantum mechanical laws that operate at a sub-atomic scale. However, very recently, a new field called 'quantum biology' has sprung up to examine the possibility of quantum effects in biological systems. This controversial work is in its infancy but might in time throw a lifeline to parapsychologists seeking to bridge the gap between mind and matter. In short, it is early days for this provocative but fascinating strand of micro-PK work.

Biological systems

Researchers interested in the possible influence of the mind on biological systems have carried out three related types of research:

the investigation of prayer, testing healers, and distant mental influence on living systems. Each will be discussed in turn.

In 1872, the British Victorian polymath Francis Galton carried out the first statistical analysis into the power of prayer. At the time, thousands of people in Britain went to church every Sunday and prayed for the well-being of the royal family. Galton hypothesized that if their prayers were effective then members of royalty should live longer than average. After scouring death records, Galton discovered that those in the royal family actually had a shorter average lifespan than those in other affluent groups, such as the landed gentry, and so concluded that prayer was ineffectual.

More recently, other researchers have taken a somewhat more systematic look at the issue. In 1988, for example, Randolph Byrd monitored the health of around four hundred patients at San Francisco General Hospital. Although the patients weren't aware of whether they were being prayed for, those who were the recipients of prayer showed significant health gains. In contrast, other studies have obtained null effects. For instance, in 2005, researchers at Duke University carried out a three-year clinical trial comparing prayer with psychological therapy. After carefully monitoring around eight hundred cardiology patients in a rigorously controlled study, the team found no beneficial effect of prayer. Perhaps unsurprisingly, meta-analyses of this inconsistent literature have produced conflicting results, depending on which studies have been included in the analysis.

Poor-quality research methodology often hampers the ability to draw conclusions. An examination of the best-quality research into the therapeutic efficacy of both intercessory prayer and remote healing on human participants was reported in the *Annals of Internal Medicine* in 2000 by John Astin of the University of Maryland School of Medicine and Elaine Harkness and Edzard Ernst of Exeter University. The researchers surveyed studies with the following indicators of methodological quality: random assignment of participants to groups; the use of placebo or other appropriate control condition; and publication in peer-reviewed journals. Of the twenty-three studies reviewed, thirteen (57%) obtained statistically significant results indicating an effect of treatment compared to the control intervention. These positive results indicate that the efficacy of prayer and healing deserves further investigation. However, despite the high quality of the reviewed studies, Astin, Harkness, and Ernst identified method-ological limitations preventing definitive conclusions from being drawn. For example, some studies did not adequately control for possible differences in participant characteristics at the outset of the study, leading to different baseline health profiles for the treatment and control groups. Another practical problem facing researchers in this area is the difficulty of establishing 'pure' control groups. For example, if a seriously ill person in a prayer study is assigned to the control group, they are still likely to be aware that friends and family are praying for them. To circum-vent this problem, researcher Larry Dossey has recommended that studies should investigate the efficacy of distant interven-tions on non-human populations.

Healers claim to be able to promote the well-being of plants and animals, and researchers have tested many of these claims. In 1959, for instance, researcher Bernard Grad from McGill University tested a Hungarian healer named Oskar Estebany. Estebany had previously been a cavalry officer and said that he had noticed that he could use his psychic energy to help heal army horses. Grad carried out a series of studies with Estebany. In one experiment, Grad removed a small area of skin from the backs of laboratory mice and then assessed the effect of Estebany's apparent healing abilities. Estebany held one group of caged mice for twenty minutes each day for eighteen days. The mice held by Estebany recovered from their wounds significantly quicker than the other mice. Other studies have examined the effects of heal-ers on blood samples, plant growth, yeast cultures, seed germination, and humans (including studies assessing hypertension, headaches, pain, and anxiety). Many of the studies have yielded positive results, but have been criticized on various grounds. For example, some critics have raised the possibility of deliberate participant fraud or inadvertent bias because the healers are often allowed to be close to (and, in some cases, to touch) experimental materials. Others have suggested that researchers are taking many different measures and only reporting those that seem to support the healer's claims.

A third strand of research has examined the possibility of distant mental influence on living systems. Much of the work in this area was carried out by parapsychologist William Braud at the Mind Science Foundation in Texas, and has involved normal volunteers rather than those claiming to be healers. Over a thirteen-year period, Braud conducted a wide variety of studies in which volunteers mentally attempted to influence a range of biological systems, including, for example, the swimming behaviour of small knife fish, and the rate of haemolysis of red blood cells in a test tube. In 1991, Braud reviewed thirty-seven of these studies and reported that the accumulated results were statistically significant.

Most of the recent work in this area has focused on two related but different forms of mental influence on the human autonomic nervous system: the remote detection of staring and mental calming (see Appendix).

Around 90% of the population have had the experience of suddenly feeling uneasy, only to turn around and discover someone staring at them. Parapsychologists have conducted a series of studies to discover if such experiences are due to psychic ability. During a typical experimental session, two volunteers are placed in separate rooms. One of the volunteers (the 'staree') has a camera placed in front of them while their physiological activity is constantly monitored. The other volunteer (the 'starer') sits in front of a television monitor that shows a live feed from the camera. At randomly determined times, the starer is asked to look at the staree's image on the monitor. Importantly, the staree is unaware of the periods when they are being stared at. At the end of the session, researchers examine the physiological data to discover whether the staree's activity was higher when the starer was looking at their image.

In 2004, Stefan Schmidt, Rainer Schneider, and Harald Walach (all from University Hospital Freiburg) and Jessica Utts (University of California, Davis) meta-analysed fifteen remote staring studies and discovered a small, but statistically significant, effect. To discover whether possible methodological flaws might account for this effect, the researchers investigated whether there was any relationship between study quality and outcome. No such relationship was found.

Other work uses a slight variation on this procedure, testing whether one person can remotely influence the physiology of another by simply thinking about them. This latter work doesn't involve the starer looking at an image of the staree, but rather simply trying to calm them down or activate them.

Stefan Schmidt's 2004 paper also included a meta-analysis of thirty-six calming/activation studies, and again found a small but significant overall effect. However, the data showed that the largest effects came from the poorest-quality studies, and that no effect of remote influence was found for the seven highest-quality studies. This analysis doesn't prove that the positive results are attributable to methodological weaknesses, but it does suggest some caution over the interpretation of the direct mental interaction studies. Schmidt and colleagues concluded that both databases show suggestive evidence in favour of remote mental interaction, but stated that future independent, high-quality studies with larger data sets are needed to confirm these findings.

In the last three chapters, we have reviewed the methods and findings of laboratory research into extrasensory perception, precognition, and psychokinesis. Over time, researchers have identified and rectified many possible methodological pitfalls, and, while results are not uniformly positive, the work cannot be easily dismissed as careless or pseudo-scientific. Parapsychologists such as Daryl Bem would like to see mainstream researchers engaging with this body of research and attempting to replicate it. One feature of parapsychological research may stand in the way of such mainstream replication effort: experimenter effects.

Experimenter effects

In 1968, Robert Rosenthal from Harvard University was one of the first psychologists to explore experimentally a strange, but important, phenomenon known as 'expectancy effects'. Rosenthal teamed up with school principal Lenore Jacobson to conduct an ingenious study demonstrating how a teacher's expectations affect the performance of their pupils. Rosenthal and Jacobson asked all of the pupils in selected classes at an elementary school to complete an IQ test. The researchers then randomly selected some of the pupils and told their teachers that the test had revealed that these pupils were expected to show rapid intellectual progress. A few months later, all of the pupils completed a second IQ test. Even though the 'gifted' pupils had been randomly selected, they generally outperformed their classmates on the second IQ test. Additional work revealed that the effect was due to teachers treating the 'gifted' kids differently by, for example, spending more time with them and giving them greater opportunities in the classroom. The work is a compelling illustration of how our expectations can create reality.

Rosenthal demonstrated that similar effects operate in psychological research, with experimenters subtly communicating their expectations to volunteers, leading them to respond in a way that fulfils the experimenter's expectations.

Similar 'experimenter effects' appear to exist in parapsychology, with some researchers consistently obtaining evidence to support the existence of psychic ability and others always obtaining chance results. These experimenter effects are seen by many parapsychologists as the major obstacle to replication in parapsychological research, but pinpointing the precise nature of the experimenter's influence is problematic. Some researchers have argued that these effects are due to the experimenter's attitude affecting the laboratory 'ambience' and volunteers' expectations. For example, in 1957, J.B. Rhine and Gaither Pratt stated that experimenters who fail to obtain positive results may be 'suspected of not ever having felt some contagious or communicable interest as would help create a favorable test environment for their subjects'. Rhine even suggested that those who did not have 'the knack' of obtaining positive results should not conduct psi research. Others, such as James Kennedy, suggest that such effects could reflect differences in research practices and competence.

To help tease apart these competing explanations, it has been suggested that researchers with a reputation for consistently producing positive effects should team up with those who tend to obtain null effects. This was accomplished in a series of studies conducted between 1999 and 2006 by Marilyn Schlitz from the Institute of Noetic Sciences in California and Richard Wiseman from the University of Hertfordshire. Schlitz believes in the existence of psychic ability and has run several studies that have yielded positive results. In contrast, Wiseman is a sceptic whose studies tend to yield null findings. Schlitz and Wiseman conducted three studies together examining the remote detection of staring. In each study, the two experimenters used the same volunteers, procedure, and equipment. The only difference was that half of the volunteers were tested by Schlitz and half by Wiseman. In the first two studies, the data from the volunteers tested by Schlitz showed a positive effect, whereas the data from those tested by Wiseman were at chance. However, in the third – and largest – study, neither experimenter obtained a psi effect.

Schlitz and Wiseman's study is a rare example of collaborative research on the question of experimenter effects. More recently, in an attempt to come up with a more definitive conclusion, Bem, Schlitz, and Arnaud Delorme from the University of California, San Diego have launched two large-scale studies using Bem's presentiment ('feeling the future') technique to assess precognition. Both studies have been pre-registered, meaning that, before any data was collected, the researchers provided a public record of their planned methods and analyses (we will discuss the importance of study registration in the next chapter). Round 1 involved thirty-two experimenters from twelve different laboratories. At the beginning, the experimenters' attitudes towards psi were measured, and the researchers predicted that those with a positive attitude would find results confirming their expectations. The prediction was not confirmed. Round 2 adjusts the planned methods and analysis in light of the findings of Round 1. Study participants will be asked to read texts that are either pro-psi or sceptical about psi, and experimenters will view either pro-psi or sceptical videos. Experimenters and participants will then have their beliefs about psi assessed. The prediction is that the pro-psi experimenters and participants will obtain evidence supporting the presentiment hypothesis, while the psi sceptics will find no such evidence. The jury is still out on the existence of experimenter effects within parapsychology, but, if they are shown to exist for certain, they will have profound implications for those hoping to develop experimental techniques that produce reliable evidence of psychic ability. Furthermore, the idea of experimenters influencing their own study outcomes would open a Pandora's box for all scientists who are attempting to conduct objective observations of data.

Conclusion

Parapsychologists interested in mental influence have carried out two very different kinds of research. One strand of the work has focused on physical systems, including the roll of dice, the output of random number generators, and even attempts to influence the behaviour of photons of light. Much of this work has yielded statistically significant results, and this is one of the few areas of experimental parapsychology that has involved researchers developing, and then testing, theories about how psychic ability might work. Most recently, this theoretical work has focused on the possible relationship between mental influence and quantum effects. The second strand of research examines possible mental influence over living systems, and includes research looking at the possible power of prayer, healing, and the remote detection of staring. Many of these studies yield evidence in favour of psychic functioning, though it is more challenging to assess outcomes and control for artefacts in this area of work, and methodological weaknesses prevent firm conclusions from being drawn even when the most carefully conducted studies are considered. By studying how the mind may interact with the physical world, from photons to patients, parapsychologists' work begins to overlap with that of physicists and clinicians. Further collaboration between parapsychologists and mainstream researchers may help to drive advances in both areas.

12
Conclusion: Parapsychology's value

When I first began exploring why people have paranormal experiences, I had little idea what to expect. The last three decades have been fascinating, challenging, and at times frustrating. It's easy to forget that very few researchers worldwide are actively conducting parapsychological research. So it's hardly surprising that progress is slow. But are parapsychologists' efforts worthwhile?

If parapsychologists can convince the scientific community of the reality of paranormal phenomena, the ramifications would be immense. We would possess an expanded understanding of human capabilities and of how consciousness interacts with the physical world, and physicists would also need to account for this in their fundamental theories. However, despite many advances in experimentation and analysis, the evidence for psychic abilities continues to be controversial. It is possible that future studies will show that psychic abilities do not exist. Does this mean that parapsychologists' efforts were fruitless? No. In fact, some historians, philosophers, and psychologists maintain that parapsychology has made substantial contributions to science and research techniques.

For instance, the philosopher Gerd Hövelmann has noted that the first behavioural science experiment ever performed using randomization and detailed statistical analysis was a parapsychological experiment into thought transference published by the Nobel Prize-winning scientist Charles Richet in 1884. These methods were later adopted or adapted by influential mainstream statisticians such as Ronald Fisher.

Early researchers in borderline topics such as homeopathy and mesmerism were also among the first to use placebos and prevent the participants and experimenters from knowing which was the experimental and which the control condition. Psychical researchers applied these methods in early tests of telepathy, before psychologists. Modern surveys have shown that parapsychologists use masked methods far more routinely than do other research areas.

Similarly, in 1940, the first example of statistical review of a body of experimental research was conducted by Pratt, Rhine, and colleagues in their review of ESP research findings. The procedure was later formalized around 1976 and given the term meta-analysis, and in 1986 methodologist Robert Rosenthal noted the contribution of parapsychologists in refining meta-analytic tools.

More recently, parapsychology has helped minimize questionable research practices (QRPs), and incidents of fraud and deception in parapsychology have typically been identified by parapsychologists themselves. Parapsychologists' measures to prevent QRPs have often been impressive (e.g. the *European Journal of Parapsychology*'s 1978 policy to review submitted papers based on the study's planned methodology, before any data had been collected) and generally precede their implementation in other fields (e.g. the Royal Society implemented such a publication policy in 2015, though only for its new journal, *Open Science*).

While it is arguably unfair to require that extraordinary claims require extraordinary evidence (see box), in many cases, parapsychology's contributions have been stimulated by the challenges of conducting well-controlled tests. As such, the investigation of claimed psychic abilities has great value in its own right.

SHOULD EXTRAORDINARY CLAIMS REQUIRE EXTRAORDINARY EVIDENCE?

Many parapsychologists argue that, if parapsychology is judged by the standards applied to any other science, it has already provided replicable evidence for psychic abilities. However, some critics maintain that, because parapsychology is testing implausible abilities for which there is currently no accepted physical mechanism, the evidential bar should be set relatively high. In other words: extraordinary claims require extraordinary evidence. This is a controversial and, some would argue, nonsensical position because judgements about the plausibility of ideas can and do change over time. However, I would argue that there is another sense in which asking for extraordinary evidence is appropriate for parapsychological claims. For whatever reason, the effects in many parapsychology experiments seem to be somewhat inconsistent and variable. I believe that seemingly fragile effects are particularly susceptible to the effects of researcher bias. Consequently, parapsychologists need to adopt and indeed develop the highest of standards.

Parapsychology is made up of three strands of work, namely: investigating strong psychic claims; examining anomalous experiences; and conducting laboratory-based experiments into the possible existence of psychic ability. We end our exploration of this controversial science with an overview of research in each of these strands, focusing on both the degree to which they support the existence of psychic abilities and their contribution to mainstream psychology.

Investigating strong psychic claims

Claims of strong psychic ability have taken many different forms, including, for example, 'thoughtography' (the ability to mentally influence photographic film), metal bending, mediumship and psychic reading, animal precognition, psychic detection, remote viewing, and telekinesis. Parapsychologists and psychical researchers have investigated these phenomena for over a century. Some researchers have focused on examining claims of macro-PK and believe that the phenomenon is genuinely paranormal. For example, psychiatrist Jule Eisenbud tested 'thoughtographer' Ted Serios and concluded that he was psychic, and mathematician John Taylor believed that Uri Geller really could use the power of his mind to bend metal. However, other researchers have argued against such conclusions, for three reasons. First, they point out that many seemingly psychic phenomena can be duplicated using magic tricks. For example, magicians have demonstrated that it's possible to produce 'thoughtographs' by using concealed devices, and sceptic James Randi has frequently employed simple magic tricks to replicate paranormal feats of metal bending. Second, sceptics note that psychics are often reluctant, or unable, to demonstrate their abilities under well-controlled conditions. In one investigation, for example, an Indian 'holy man' was unable to produce any paranormal phenomena whenever test conditions prevented sleight-of-hand. Finally, studies of physical mediums often uncover trickery, which led psychical researchers to shift to the study of mental mediums, who purportedly provide information from deceased individuals. A few mental mediums, such as Leonora Piper, have convinced even sceptical researchers that they possess psychic abilities. However, when researchers began to implement better-controlled tests on individuals claiming strong ESP abilities, they found little, if any, evidence to support the existence of such abilities. For example, Dutch parapsychologist Henk Boerenkamp conducted a large-scale project examining the accuracy of psychic readers and found no evidence of genuine paranormal ability. Likewise, psychologist Harvey Irwin's research into psychic detectives revealed that they were no more accurate than university students.

Although this strand of work on the whole has not revealed compelling evidence of psychic ability, it has made several significant contributions to mainstream psychology. Research into séance phenomena has revealed considerable insights into the psychology of eyewitness testimony, including how witnesses omit important details, are influenced by the power of suggestion, and alter their accounts over time. Exposés of those claiming macro-PK abilities have helped identify some of the stratagems used by skilled deceivers to manipulate observers' attention, perception, and memory. Research into psychic reading has uncovered how 'cold-reading' techniques give the illusion that psychics know a great deal about complete strangers, including how they fish for information, employ stereotyping, use verbal and non-verbal feedback, and formulate statements that appear specific but are actually endorsed by the majority of people. Finally, studies into the psychic powers of non-human animals have expanded our understanding of these animals' remarkable sensitivity to both non-verbal signals from humans and subtle environmental cues.

Anomalous experiences

Surveys show that psychic experiences are commonly reported and this has stimulated research not only by parapsychologists, but also by psychologists, neuroscientists, and clinicians. They are seeking to understand and explain such experiences including dream precognition, ghosts and hauntings, out-of-body experiences (OBEs), and near-death experiences (NDEs).

Four very different approaches have been used to study whether such experiences constitute evidence of the paranormal. First, early work in the area involved weighing people at the moment of death in the hope of detecting a sudden weight loss as the soul vacated the body. Unfortunately, this work was affected by methodological problems, with some suggesting that the researchers were actually detecting a loss in bodily fluids.

Second, researchers studying OBEs have asked volunteers to try to float away from their bodies and determine the nature of a hidden target, such as a photograph or a list of numbers. Similarly, parapsychologists examining NDEs have placed targets on shelves above head height in hospital wards to test the hypothesis that patients who report leaving their body during NDEs might be able to determine the identity of the targets. Neither type of study has yielded strong evidence of psychic ability. The successful identification of targets during OBE experiments has occurred under suspicious circumstances, and hospital patients have yet to identify correctly any of the targets.

Third, a small number of researchers have attempted to determine whether ghosts and apparitions actually exist. The bulk of this work was carried out around the turn of the twentieth century by leading figures within the Society for Psychical Research. This survey-based research involved collecting apparitional accounts from a large number of people and then attempting to determine whether such experiences could have had a normal explanation. Unfortunately, there is no easy way of assessing the reliability and accuracy of the accounts; therefore, although the amount of evidence is impressive, the quality of the reports is always open to question.

Fourth, research conducted by parapsychologist Gertrude Schmeidler and colleagues in the 1960s and 1970s involved asking mediums to tour haunted locations and describe the ghosts that they believed were there. Their reports frequently matched accounts provided by eyewitnesses who claimed to have experienced the ghosts. Schmeidler's work is innovative, intriguing, and deserving of greater attention. However, more recent work has demonstrated that reports of ghostly experiences are reliably associated with aspects of people's surroundings (including, for example, lighting levels and the size of spaces), and so the similarity between the mediums' and eyewitnesses' reports may have been due to both groups responding to the same cues.

However, parapsychological research into anomalous experiences has made a considerable contribution to mainstream psychology. Studies have suggested that many psychic experiences may be attributable not to paranormal factors, but to the operation of four main psychological mechanisms: unconscious cognition, poor probability judgements, propensity to find correspondences, and selective memory. There is considerable experimental evidence to support the existence of each of these mechanisms, and some recent work suggests that many of them (especially propensity to find correspondences) may explain why those who believe in the paranormal are especially prone to such experiences. Parapsychologists have also demonstrated that similar cognitive processes can bias how those with a strong *disbelief* in the paranormal evaluate evidence conflicting with their beliefs.

However, perhaps most progress in understanding has been made by researchers studying the psychology and neuropsychology of OBEs and NDEs. This work has taken four very different forms. First, psychologists have demonstrated that OBEs and NDEs are strongly associated with a series of psychological measures, including dissociation, fantasy proneness, hypnotic susceptibility, and absorption. Second, studies using the 'false rubber hand' paradigm and virtual-reality techniques have both revealed how people construct a sense of where they are, and demonstrated that it is surprisingly easy to persuade people that they have left their bodies. Third, neuroscientists have started to uncover a neurological explanation for these experiences, noting that disruption to the temporo-parietal region of the brain results in OBE-like sensations. Finally, findings from work showing that people from different cultures report differing types of NDEs have provided a vivid insight into the power of culture and expectation to shape experience.

In short, research into anomalous experiences has not yielded compelling evidence of the paranormal. This may be due, in part, to difficulties in eliciting such experiences under closely controlled conditions. However, the work has contributed a great deal to mainstream psychology and neuroscience, and has started to uncover many of the psychological and neurological mechanisms that underpin such experiences.

Laboratory-based investigations

Recognizing the limitations of spontaneous paranormal experiences and of work with psychic claimants, the majority of parapsychologists seeking to provide compelling evidence regarding putative psychic abilities have turned to laboratory-based methods. This strand of parapsychological research involves conducting experiments into the possible existence of ESP and PK. This approach dates back to the turn of the twentieth century, but began in earnest with the work of Joseph Banks Rhine at Duke University. Much of Rhine's work into ESP involved volunteers attempting to guess the identity of hidden Zener cards, while his research exploring PK involved their trying to mentally influence the roll of dice. Rhine and his associates conducted hundreds of thousands of trials and believed that his results supported the existence of both ESP and PK. Perhaps unsurprisingly, critics were sceptical about aspects of this work, arguing, for example, that many of the studies employed insufficient measures against possible cheating and questionable statistical procedures. This debate was as heated as it was complex.

Eventually, parapsychologists moved away from Rhine's card-guessing and dice-rolling experiments, and developed new testing procedures. Starting in the 1960s, researchers Montague Ullman and Stanley Krippner, from the Maimonides Dream Laboratory in New York, carried out a series of studies into the possible existence of dream telepathy and precognition. The studies yielded positive results that seemed to provide evidence for ESP. Some researchers such as Irvin Child questioned both the methodology and statistical procedures employed during the studies. However, Child also pointed out that many psychologists' criticisms of the Maimonides studies were unfair and shoddy.

Nevertheless, the general notion of testing volunteers while they are in an altered state of consciousness stood the test of time. From the 1970s onwards, one of the most widely used methods for studying telepathy involved the ganzfeld procedure, which involves placing one volunteer in a mild state of sensory isolation and then asking them to describe whatever thoughts and images flow through their mind. Meanwhile, a second volunteer in a separate room is asked to look at a picture postcard or film clip, and psychically send it to the other volunteer.

In the 1980s, parapsychologist Charles Honorton and sceptical psychologist Ray Hyman conducted a lengthy debate about the results of these studies. Much of this work involved several meta-analyses (a statistical technique used to combine the results from a large number of studies), with Honorton arguing that the findings supported the existence of ESP and Hyman arguing that this was not the case. Eventually, the pair authored a set of methodological guidelines for future work in the area. These guidelines improved the quality of subsequent studies, although the results of this work are still the topic of fierce debate between proponents and critics.

Addressing questionable research practices in parapsychology and beyond

There is little doubt that over time the various methodological debates have identified potential problems with the procedures used by parapsychologists. For example, critics have suggested that parapsychologists have unconsciously inflated their results by using several statistical analyses to analyse their data and then reporting only the one that provides evidence of ESP, continuing to collect data until they get a desired result, and not reporting studies with negative findings. Of course, the same questionable research practices (QRPs) could also cause researchers who do not favour the ESP hypothesis to unconsciously underplay their findings, and choose statistical procedures that support the non-existence of ESP, to run studies until they obtain a null result, and fail to publish studies that obtain positive findings. It would also be tempting but wrong to conclude from this discussion that only parapsychology is susceptible to QRPs. Many other mainstream areas face similar issues and parapsychology has been praised for being comparatively quick to recognize and attempt to tackle such issues.

Such debates have also identified potential limitations of meta-analysis. Meta-analyses tend to be conducted after the results of individual studies have been published. Therefore, proponents of ESP may choose to include studies that obtain positive results and exclude those that don't, while sceptics may choose to do the exact opposite.

However, on a more constructive note, the methodological debates have also resulted in various ways of minimizing these problems. Perhaps the most important of these involves study registration, wherein researchers provide a record of their intended work before carrying out the study. In the case of individual studies, registration includes, for example, researchers noting their intended statistical analysis and number of volunteers. Researchers intending to conduct a meta-analysis need to register several aspects of their work, including the criteria that will be used to select studies and the statistical analyses that will be used to combine the results of this work. To prevent bias, this should ideally be done before the results of the individual studies are known.

It is revealing and somewhat shocking to see what happens when study registration is implemented in other areas of research such as healthcare. For example, in 2015, Robert Kaplan, a researcher for the US Department of Health and Human Services, investigated the results of large-scale randomized controlled trials funded by the National Heart, Lung, and Blood Institute after clinicaltrials.gov, in 2000, introduced requirements for transparent study registration and reporting. Pre-2000, 57% of studies reported a significant benefit of interventions aimed at reducing cardiovascular disease. After 2000, only 8% of trials reported significant benefits. This suggests that the picture from the pre-2000 studies was distorted by researchers selectively reporting analyses favourable to the intervention being tested.

Compared to healthcare research, parapsychology is a relatively minuscule and poorly resourced field, so it is a challenge to establish and maintain procedures to minimize QRPs. It has done well to introduce initiatives such as the *European Journal of Parapsychology*'s 1978 editorial policy, and there are recent signs of more widespread use of procedures to minimize QRPs. In the late 1990s, three parapsychology laboratories staged a coordinated attempt to replicate a series of studies that had apparently obtained evidence for micro-PK. All of the work was registered. In 2012, James Kennedy and I set up the first public registration system in parapsychology. Now any parapsychologist can quickly place on record the details of their studies prior to their carrying out the work. For example, in 2011, Daryl Bem reported a series of studies that appeared to support the existence of precognition. Bem is currently coordinating a second multi-centre attempt to replicate this work, and both replication programmes have been registered on our study registry.

The methodological debates in parapsychology have also raised issues that are highly relevant to mainstream psychology. For example, in 2012, Stanford University medical researcher John Ioannidis estimated that a shocking 53% of published findings in mainstream psychology have not been replicated and so may be spurious. In 2015, the journal *Science* published the results of a large-scale 'reproducibility project' that addressed Ioannidis's concerns. Led by Virginia University's Brian Nosek, a team of 270 researchers repeated 100 psychology experiments that had previously reported positive results. Only 36% of the original findings were confirmed. Having now recognized the value of study registration, many psychology journals are revising their publication guidelines to encourage such practices. Kennedy and I have published recommendations for improved study registration practice in psychology, based on our experience with parapsychological study registration. Psychologists, such as Eric-Jan Wagenmakers of University of Amsterdam, have acknowledged the contribution that parapsychologists have made to raising awareness of these methodological issues.

The laboratory-based approach to parapsychology provides perhaps the best evidence for psychic ability. Over time, the methodological quality of these studies has increased, and many parapsychologists believe that the findings have remained both positive and convincing. The majority of researchers argue that, at the very least, the results clearly justify the need for additional research. There is also no doubt from laboratory-based testing of hypothesized ESP and PK abilities that accusations that this work is pseudo-scientific are ill informed. However, various problems remain and it is only very recently that researchers have started to create procedures that will help eliminate these issues. As we've seen, the evidential standards demanded for parapsychological studies generally exceed those applied to less controversial topics. This may be justifiable not because of the extraordinary nature of the claim that is being tested by parapsychologists, but because the effects in psi studies seem to be rather fragile and inconsistent, so they may be particularly vulnerable to researcher bias. In my view, parapsychologists should embrace and promote these high standards, and lead the way for other disciplines facing replication challenges. As we have seen, parapsychology has a long and distinguished history of pioneering methodological and conceptual advances that have benefited science. Making study registration the norm may become the next example of excellent practice in parapsychology.

Will this next phase of laboratory-based ESP and PK research finally provide researchers with solid evidence of psychic ability? Or will the studies confirm the sceptics' suspicions and obtain negative results? There is no way of knowing at the moment. As is so often the case in such controversial areas, the only way forward is to carry out carefully the necessary work and be guided by the data. One thing is more certain though. Whatever the outcome of such experiments, people will always have experiences that they believe are paranormal, and the study of these experiences will, one way or another, help extend the frontiers of knowledge.

Appendix: How to test for ESP and PK ability

This Appendix outlines both formal and informal experiments that you can use to test for ESP and PK using materials that you can easily find at home. In addition to being interesting and fun, carrying out such experiments will highlight some of the pitfalls that have hindered past parapsychology experiments, and the ways in which researchers have overcome these issues.

ESP card guessing

Informal clairvoyance test

This ESP test requires a deck of playing cards and four slips of paper. Discard the court cards (the Jacks, Queens, and Kings), leaving you with forty cards – ten Diamonds, ten Spades, ten Hearts, and ten Clubs. Next, write the name of one suit (either 'Diamonds', 'Spades', 'Hearts', or 'Clubs') on the separate slips of paper, and place the four slips in a row on a table (see Figure 4).

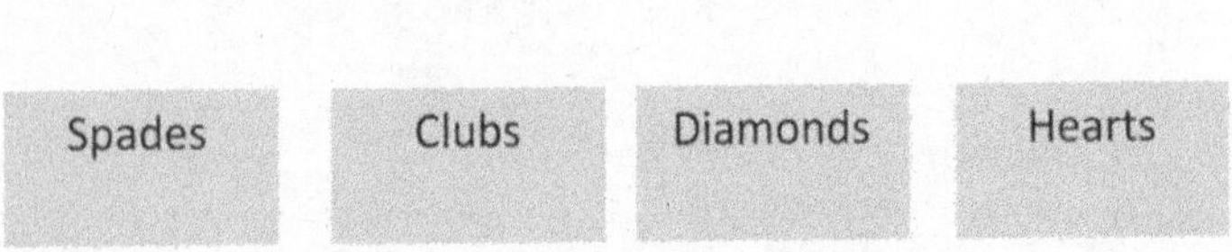

Spades	Clubs	Diamonds	Hearts

Figure 4 Set-up for clairvoyance test

Shuffle the deck of cards face down and deal off the top card. Without looking at the face of the card, guess the suit of the card, and then place it face down on the appropriate slip of paper. If, for example, you think the top card is a Diamond, you would place it on the slip of paper labelled 'Diamonds'. Work your way through the rest of the deck repeating the procedure, ending up with four piles of face-down cards (see Figure 5).

Next, turn over each pile and count how many correct guesses (known as 'hits') there are in each pile. For example, if there are eight cards in the 'Spades' pile, but only three of them are actually Spades, then this would count as three hits. Finally, add up the number of hits in each pile to create an overall total.

As there are four suits, the likelihood of correctly guessing the suit of each playing card by chance alone is one in four. Because you made forty guesses, you should obtain around ten

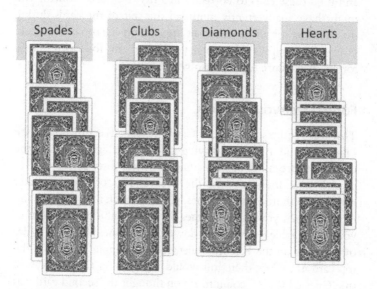

Figure 5 Laying out the cards against your guesses

hits simply by chance. According to the laws of probability, you would obtain fifteen hits by chance 5% of the time (what this means is that, if you repeated this experiment a hundred times you would obtain fifteen hits five times just by chance); seventeen hits would occur only 1% of the time (i.e. only once in 100 times); and nineteen hits would occur only 0.1% of the time (1 in 1,000). All of these would be seen as high scores.

However, parapsychologists probably wouldn't be too impressed if someone obtained a high score, because there are four main problems with this test. First, even though high scores are, by definition, improbable, they do occasionally happen by chance. Second, your informal shuffling may not have properly mixed up the deck. Third, if you have previously played with the deck, you might have unconsciously known that certain cards have subtle creases or other marks on the back of them, and used these cues to correctly identify the cards. Fourth, you might have inadvertently glimpsed the suit of the cards during the shuffling, or when you dealt the card off the top of the deck. However, parapsychologists have devised the following, more formal, procedure to help resolve these issues.

Formal clairvoyance test

This test requires a friend, a Card-guessing Record Sheet (see Figure 6), and a deck of playing cards. Once again, discard the court cards from the deck, leaving you with forty cards.

Ask your friend to take the deck and its box into another room, riffle shuffle it seven times, place the deck into the box, and return. When your friend comes back, place the box in front of you on the table. Next, write down your guesses about the order of the cards on the Record Sheet. If, for example, you think the top card is a Club, then you would write 'C' in the first row of the 'Guessed Order' column. If you thought the second card was a Spade, then you would write 'S' in the second row. And so

Card Number	Guessed Order (C, H, S, or D)	Actual Order (C, H, S, or D)	Hit or Miss? (1 or 0)
1			
2			
3			
4			
5			
6			
7			
8			
9			
10			
11			
12			
13			
14			
15			
16			
17			
18			
19			
20			
21			
22			
23			
24			
25			
26			
27			
28			
29			
30			
31			
32			
33			
34			
35			
36			
37			
38			
39			
40			
TOTAL			

Figure 6 Card-guessing Record Sheet

on through the deck. Once you have made your forty guesses, remove the cards from the box and carefully record the order of the cards in the 'Actual Order' column of the Record Sheet.

Finally, compare the two columns, giving yourself one point in the 'Hits' column each time you score a match. Add up the total number of hits and write this in the shaded box at the bottom of the table.

This procedure overcomes many of the problems with the informal test. Riffle shuffling the cards seven times will properly mix them up. Also, placing the cards in the box means that you couldn't have been influenced by any marks on them, or glimpsed the faces of a card. Finally, the likelihood of obtaining another high score on this second test simply by chance alone is very low (although not impossible!). As a result, repeatedly obtaining fifteen or more hits under these more formal conditions would be seen as more compelling evidence of clairvoyance.

Informal telepathy test

This test involves your friend, the deck of cards, and four slips of paper. Once again, discard the court cards from the deck, write the name of one suit on each of the separate slips of paper, and place the four slips in a row on a table.

Ask your friend to sit on the opposite side of the table and face you. They are going to be the 'sender' and you are going to be the 'receiver'. Hand the deck to your friend and ask them to shuffle it face down. Next, instruct them to deal off the top card, hold it up so that they can see the face of the card and you can see its back, and concentrate on the suit of the card.

Make a guess about the suit of the card, and ask your friend to place the card face down on the appropriate slip of paper. For example, if you think the card is a Diamond, say the word 'Diamond', and have your friend place the card on the piece of paper marked 'Diamond'. Work your way through the deck repeating this procedure.

To score the test, count how many hits you have in each stack, and then add up all of your hits. You would expect to obtain around ten hits by chance, and fifteen or more would be seen as a high score.

Although this test is easy and fun, it suffers from the same kinds of problems as the informal clairvoyance test. For example, the shuffling may not have properly mixed up the cards, and you may have glimpsed the cards as your friend was handling them. Parapsychologists have overcome these issues by developing the following formal test.

Formal telepathy test

This test involves your friend, a deck of cards, the Card-guessing Record Sheet, and two stopwatches. Once again, discard the court cards from the deck. Your friend is going to be the 'sender' and you are going to be the 'receiver'.

Start both of the stopwatches at the same time, and hand one of them to your friend. Ask your friend to go to another room and riffle shuffle the deck seven times. Then, when their stopwatch indicates 'three minutes', ask them to deal off the top card and concentrate on it. At exactly the same time, you should record your guess on the Record Sheet. Then, fifteen seconds later, your friend should look at the second card and you should make your second guess. Once all forty guesses have been recorded, your friend should join you and record the actual order of the cards on the Record Sheet.

Finally, add up your number of hits. Repeatedly obtaining fifteen or more hits under these more formal conditions would be seen as more compelling evidence of telepathy.

Free-response telepathy test

The previous tests involved trying to guess the suits of playing cards. These types of tests are often referred to as 'forced choice', because you only have a limited range of response options. In the following 'free-response' tests, you will describe whatever thoughts or images go through your mind, and then compare these impressions with a picture.

Informal telepathy test

This test involves your friend, two clipboards, two sheets of paper, and two pencils. Your friend is going to be the 'sender' and you are going to be the 'receiver'.

Place the pieces of paper on the clipboards, and then hand one clipboard to your friend. Ask them to make any sketch on the paper without showing it to you. When they have finished, ask your friend to concentrate on their drawing. Pick up your clipboard and draw whatever comes to mind. Try to resist interpreting any shapes and images that come into your mind. For example, if you see two circles side by side, just draw two circles – don't be tempted to label these as a bicycle or a pair of spectacles.

Once you have completed your drawing, compare it with your friend's drawing. Are there any strong similarities? Even if there are, this is not necessarily evidence of telepathy. Such correspondences can occur by chance, or might be due to both of you sharing the same interests (perhaps, for example, you both drew a flower because you both like gardening). To rule out these possible problems, parapsychologists have developed the following, more formal, procedure.

Formal telepathy test

This experiment requires your friend, access to the web and a printer, and two envelopes.

Before the experiment, your friend should download four pictures from the web, making sure that you don't see any of the pictures. They should try to make the pictures as different from one another as possible. For instance, if one picture depicts water, they should try to avoid having water in any of the other three pictures. Next, your friend should print out postcard-sized copies of each picture, and number them 1 to 4 (this is referred to as the 'Sending Pack'). Finally, they should print out a second copy of the four pictures, and place these copies into an opaque envelope (this is called the 'Judging Pack').

Your friend is going to be the 'sender' and you are going to be the 'receiver'. During the study, your friend takes the Sending Pack into another room, and you have the envelope containing the Judging Pack. Your friend then uses the Random Number Table (see Figure 7) to select one of the four images. To do this, they need to close their eyes and place their finger anywhere on the table. They then open their eyes, look at the number nearest to their finger, and then apply the following rule:

If the random number is 1 or 5, choose Picture 1.
If the random number is 2 or 6, choose Picture 2.
If the random number is 3 or 7, choose Picture 3.
If the random number is 4 or 8, choose Picture 4.

If the random number is 0 or 9, ignore it and move to the next number in the row.

Your friend then looks at the chosen picture for ten minutes, trying to communicate it mentally to you. Meanwhile, you sit in a comfortable chair, perhaps play some relaxing music, and allow any thoughts and impressions to drift through your mind for ten minutes. Make a note or sketch of these impressions. Then, open the envelope containing the 'Judging Pack', carefully compare your impressions with each of the four pictures, and choose the picture that best matches your thoughts and feelings.

Once you have made a note of your decision, ask your friend to come back into the room with the picture that they were concentrating on. If your chosen picture matches their picture, then you have scored a hit. Otherwise the session is a miss. The likelihood of your choosing the correct picture by chance alone is one in four. If you repeat the experiment ten times, using a different set of four pictures each time, six or more hits would be considered a high score. For twenty trials, you need nine or more hits.

```
11164 36318 75061 37674 26320 75100 10431 20418 19228 91792
21215 91791 76831 58678 87054 31687 93205 43685 19732 08468
10438 44482 66558 37649 08882 90870 12462 41810 01806 02977
36792 26236 33266 66583 60881 97395 20461 36742 02852 50564
73944 04773 12032 51414 82384 38370 00249 80709 72605 67497

49563 12872 14063 93104 78483 72717 68714 18048 25005 04151
64208 48237 41701 73117 33242 42314 83049 21933 92813 04763
51486 72875 38605 29341 80749 80151 33835 52602 79147 08868
99756 26360 64516 17971 48478 09610 04638 17141 09227 10606
71325 55217 13015 72907 00431 45117 33827 92873 02953 85474

65285 97198 12138 53010 94601 15838 16805 61004 43516 17020
17264 57327 38224 29301 31381 38109 34976 65692 98566 29550
95639 99754 31199 92558 68368 04985 51092 37780 40261 14479
61555 76404 86210 11808 12841 45147 97438 60022 12645 62000
78137 98768 04689 87130 79225 08153 84967 64539 79493 74917

62490 99215 84987 28759 19177 14733 24550 28067 68894 38490
24216 63444 21283 07044 92729 37284 13211 37485 10415 36457
16975 95428 33226 55903 31605 43817 22250 03918 46999 98501
59138 39542 71168 57609 91510 77904 74244 50940 31553 62562
29478 59652 50414 31966 87912 87154 12944 49862 96566 48825

96155 95009 27429 72918 08457 78134 48407 26061 58754 05326
29621 66583 62966 12468 20245 14015 04014 35713 03980 03024
12639 75291 71020 17265 41598 64074 64629 63293 53307 48766
14544 37134 54714 02401 63228 26831 19386 15457 17999 18306
83403 88827 09834 11333 68431 31706 26652 04711 34593 22561
```

Figure 7 Random Number Table

Micro-PK and Bio-PK tests

Parapsychologists have investigated the idea that mental intention can influence both physical objects and living organisms. The first area of research is known as micro-PK, and examines whether it is possible to mentally influence small objects such as the roll of dice. The second area of research is known as bio-PK, and includes tests of whether people can detect when they are being stared at.

Informal micro-PK test

This test requires one die. Choose a number between one and six, and write this 'target number' on the Informal Micro-PK Record Sheet (see Figure 8). Next, shake the die between your hands and then roll it onto a table. If your target number comes up, place a tick in the 'Hit' column of the first row. Repeat this process thirty-six times, then add up your hits and write this total at the bottom of the table. Because there are six possible outcomes of each roll, the likelihood of obtaining a hit by chance alone is one in six. Over thirty-six rolls, you should get six hits just by chance. Eleven or more hits would be considered a high score.

There are, however, two main problems with this informal test. First, in most dice, the pips are scooped out from the surface of the dice. The 'one' face has less material scooped out than the 'six' face, making it heavier. Over a large number of rolls, there will be a slight bias, causing the heavier 'one' face to end up at the bottom of the die and the lighter 'six' face to end up uppermost more of the time. Second, shaking the die between your hands doesn't ensure that the throw will be random. Parapsychologists have developed more formal testing procedures to overcome these problems.

My target number is _____	
Roll Number	Hit
1	
2	
3	
4	
5	
6	
7	
8	
9	
10	
11	
12	
13	
14	
15	
16	
17	
18	
19	
20	
21	
22	
23	
24	
25	
26	
27	
28	
29	
30	
31	
32	
33	
34	
35	
36	
TOTAL	

Figure 8 Informal Micro-PK Record Sheet

Formal micro-PK test

In the previous informal test, you decided your target number. In this formal test, the target number systematically changes throughout the test (see Figure 9). This overcomes any concerns about the die being biased. To overcome the possibility of the throw being biased, shake the die in a cup and make sure that it rebounds off a hard vertical surface, such as a wall.

Use the Formal Micro-PK Record Sheet to make a note every time you get a hit, and then add up the number of hits and enter it at the bottom of the sheet.

Over the course of thirty-six rolls, you would expect around six hits by chance, with a high score being eleven or more hits. Consistently obtaining high scores over several runs would be consistent with the existence of psychokinesis.

Remote staring detection

This test is based on one of the most commonly reported types of psychic experience – the sense of being stared at.

Informal remote staring test

This test requires a friend and a bell. Your friend will act as the 'sender' and you will be the 'receiver'. Ask your friend to sit about six feet behind you, facing your back. When you are ready to start the experiment, say the word 'start'. Your friend then decides whether the first trial is a 'Stare' or 'No Stare' trial, and then records their decision on the Sender Record Sheet (see Figure 10a).

If your friend chooses a Stare trial, then they should look at your back for fifteen seconds. If they decide it is a No Stare trial, then they should look down for fifteen seconds. Either way, at the end of the trial, the sender should ring the bell. You should then decide whether or not you were being stared at and record your decision on the Receiver Record Sheet (see Figure 10b).

This procedure is repeated for all twenty trials.

Roll Number	Hit
Target number = 1	
1	
2	
3	
4	
5	
6	
Target number = 2	
7	
8	
9	
10	
11	
12	
Target number = 3	
13	
14	
15	
16	
17	
18	
Target number = 4	
19	
20	
21	
22	
23	
24	
Target number = 5	
25	
26	
27	
28	
29	
30	
Target number = 6	
31	
32	
33	
34	
35	
36	
TOTAL	

Figure 9 Formal Micro-PK Record Sheet

Trial Number	Trial Type Stare ('S') or No Stare ('NS')
1	
2	
3	
4	
5	
6	
7	
8	
9	
10	
11	
12	
13	
14	
15	
16	
17	
18	
19	
20	

Figure 10a Sender Record Sheet

To score the test, compare the Sender Record Sheet with the Receiver Record Sheet, and give yourself one mark whenever you correctly guessed whether a trial involved staring or not staring. Enter the total number of hits at the bottom of the Receiver Record Sheet.

Because there were two types of trial (Stare and No Stare), the likelihood of being correct by chance alone is one in two. With twenty trials, you should obtain about ten hits by chance; fifteen or more hits would be seen as a high score. However, the test has two main problems. First, your friend may have fidgeted more when they weren't staring, and you might have unconsciously detected these noises and used them to figure out that it was a No Stare trial. Also, you may have been able to guess when your friend decided to stare or look away because you know how they tend to think. Parapsychologists have devised various ways of overcoming these problems in more formal tests.

Trial Number	Guess Stare ('S') or No Stare ('NS')	Hit
1		
2		
3		
4		
5		
6		
7		
8		
9		
10		
11		
12		
13		
14		
15		
16		
17		
18		
19		
20		
TOTAL		

Figure 10b Receiver Record Sheet

Formal remote staring test

Any formal test involves two key elements.

First, it is important to prevent any sensory cues between you and your friend. For instance, you could sit on one side of a double-glazed window with your back to the window, and your friend could sit on the other side of the window. Better still, set up a webcam that sends a live image of you to a television monitor in another room, and have your friend stare at the image or look away from it. To coordinate the trials without the use of a bell, ensure that you and your friend each have a stopwatch. Synchronize the stopwatches at the start of the experiment and then conduct a trial every twenty seconds.

Second, it is important to ensure that the order of Stare and No Stare trials is random. Your friend can do this by using the

Random Number Table to determine whether a trial involves staring. They can do this by closing their eyes and pointing at a number in the table. An even number (0,2,4,6,8) results in a Stare trial and an odd number (1,3,5,7,9) results in a No Stare trial.

Online tests

Aside from the above simple procedures that you can carry out with materials from your own home, several websites exist that invite you to participate in online experiments and games exploring your psychic abilities. Try the following sites from Rupert Sheldrake and the Institute of Noetic Sciences:

http://www.sheldrake.org/participate

http://noetic.org/research/participate/online-activities

Further reading

The publications below vary in their technical detail. In a few cases, links to scientific journal articles are given. Typically, the Methods and Results sections of such articles are too technical for the lay reader. However, these parts can be skipped in favour of the Abstract, Introduction, and Discussion sections, which are generally more accessible.

Chapter 1: Introduction: The roots of parapsychology

Beloff, J. 1993. *Parapsychology: A Concise History*. London, Athlone Press.

Chapter 2: Macro-PK

Braude, S.E. 2007. *The Gold Leaf Lady and Other Parapsychological Investigations*. Chicago, University of Chicago Press.

Lamont, P. 2005. *The First Psychic: The Peculiar Mystery of a Notorious Victorian Wizard*. London, Little, Brown.

Polidoro, M. 2007. The magic in the brain: How conjuring works to deceive our minds. In S. Della Sala (Ed.) *Tall Tales About the Mind and Brain: Separating Fact from Fiction*. Oxford, Oxford University Press.

Wiseman, R. and Morris, R.L. 1995. *Guidelines for Testing Psychic Claimants*. Hatfield, University of Hertfordshire Press.

Chapter 3: Psychic reading, remote viewing and telepathic animals: ESP outside the lab

Christopher, M. 1971. *Seers, Psychics and ESP*. London, Cassell.

May, E.C. 1996. The American Institutes for Research Review of the Department of Defense's STAR GATE Program: A Commentary. *Journal of Parapsychology*, *60*, 3–23. (Edwin May's response to the AIR report on the Star Gate remote viewing project. Available at: http://www.lfr.org/lfr/csl/media/air_mayresponse.html)

Rowland, I. 2008. *The Full Facts Book of Cold Reading*. London, Ian Rowland Ltd.

Sheldrake, R. 1999. *Dogs That Know When Their Owners are Coming Home and Other Unexplained Powers of Animals*. London, Arrow.

Wiseman, R. Outline of the exchange between Sheldrake and Wiseman over Jaytee, with links to individual articles. Available at: http://www.richardwiseman.com/Jaytee.html

Chapter 4: Mediumship and survival

Angoff, A. 1974. *Eileen Garrett and the World Beyond the Senses*. New York, William Morrow.

Braude, S.E. 2003. *Immortal Remains: The Evidence for Life After Death*. Maryland, Rowman and Littlefield.

Lamont, P. 2005. *The First Psychic: The Peculiar Mystery of a Notorious Victorian Wizard*. London, Little, Brown.

Mills, A. and Tucker, J.B. 2014. Past-life experiences. In E. Cardeña, S.J. Lynn, and S. Krippner (Eds) *Varieties of Anomalous Experience: Examining the Scientific Evidence*, 2nd ed. Washington, DC, American Psychological Association.

Oppenheim, J. 1988. *The Other World: Spiritualism and Psychical Research in England, 1850–1914*. Cambridge, Cambridge University Press.

Tanner, A.E. 1910. *Studies in Spiritism*. New York, D. Appleton & Co.

Chapter 5: Out-of-body experiences

Blackmore, S. 1982. *Beyond the Body: An Investigation of Out-of-the-Body Experiences*. London, Heinemann.

Blanke, O., Ortigue, S., Landis, T., and Seeck, M. 2002. Stimulating illusory own-body perceptions. *Nature, 419*, 269–70. Available at: https://hpenlaboratory.uchicago.edu/sites/cacioppoNeurolab.uchicago.edu/files/uploads/Ortigue_Nature 2002.pdf

Irwin, H. 1985. *Flight of Mind: A Psychological Study of the Out-Of-Body Experience*. Metuchen, NJ: Scarecrow Press.

Chapter 6: Near-death experiences

Augustine, K. (2015). Near-death experiences are hallucinations. In M. Martin and K. Augustine (Eds) *The Myth of an Afterlife: The Case Against Life After Death*. Lanham, Maryland, Rowman & Littlefield.

Greyson, B. 2014. Near-death experiences. In E. Cardeña, S.J. Lynn, and S. Krippner (Eds) *Varieties of Anomalous Experience: Examining the Scientific Evidence*, 2nd ed. Washington, DC, American Psychological Association.

Ring, K. 1980. *Life at Death: A Scientific Investigation of the Near-Death Experience*. New York, Coward, McCann and Geoghegan.

Chapter 7: Hauntings and apparitions

Houran, J. and Lange, R. (Eds) 2001. *Hauntings and Poltergeists: Multidisciplinary Perspectives*. Jefferson, NC, McFarland.

Available at: *Science of Ghosts* website: http://www.scienceofghosts.com/

Wiseman, R., Watt, C., Stevens, P., Greening, E., and O'Keeffe, C. 2003. An investigation into alleged 'hauntings'. *British Journal of Psychology*, *94*(2), 195–211. Available at: https://koestlerunit.wordpress.com/research-overview/archive-of-kpu-publications-by-author/

Chapter 8: The psychology of psychic experiences

Diaconis, P. and Mosteller, F. 1989. Methods for studying coincidences. *Journal of the American Statistical Association*, *84*, 853–61. Available at: http://www.math.northwestern.edu/~fcale/CCC/DC.pdf

Marks, D. and Kammann, R. 1980. *The Psychology of the Psychic*. Amherst New York, Prometheus Books.

Simmonds-Moore, C. 2012. *Exceptional Experiences and Health: Essays on Mind, Body and Human Potential*. New Jersey, McFarland.

Chapter 9: Telepathy and clairvoyance in the laboratory

Kennedy, J.E. 2013. Can parapsychology move beyond the controversies of retrospective meta-analyses? *Journal of Parapsychology*, 77, 21–35. Available at: jeksite.org/psi/jp13a.pdf

Koestler Parapsychology Unit Registry for Parapsychological Experiments. Available at: https://koestlerunit.wordpress.com/study-registry/

Rosenthal, R. 1986. Meta-analytic procedures and the nature of replication: The ganzfeld debate. *Journal of Parapsychology*, *50*, 315–36.

Ullman, M., Krippner, S., with Vaughan, A. 1973. *Dream Telepathy: Experiments in Nocturnal ESP*, Jefferson, NC, McFarland.

Chapter 10: Precognition in the laboratory

Bem, D.J. 2011. Feeling the future: Experimental evidence for anomalous retroactive influences on cognition and affect. *Journal of Personality and Social Psychology*, *100*, 407–25. Available at: http://dbem.ws/FeelingFuture.pdf

Radin, D.I. 1997. Unconscious perception of future emotions: An experiment in presentiment. *Journal of Scientific Exploration*, *11*, 163–80. Available at: https://www.scientificexploration.org/journal/volume-11-number-2-1997

Ritchie, S., Wiseman, R., and French, C. 2012. Replication, replication, replication. *The Psychologist*, *25*, 346–57. Available at: http://thepsychologist.bps.org.uk/archive

Chapter 11: Mental influence in the laboratory: Physical and biological

Astin, J.A., Harkness, E., and Ernst, E. 2000. The efficacy of 'distant healing': A systematic review of randomized trials. *Annals of Internal Medicine*, *132*, 903–10. Available at: https://online.stat.psu.edu/~rho/mindon/distant.pdf

Dunne, B.J., Nelson, R.D., and Jahn, R.G. 1988. Operator-related anomalies in a random mechanical cascade. *Journal of Scientific Exploration*, *2*, 155–79. Available at: http://www.princeton.edu/~pear/pdfs/1988-operator-related-anomalies-rmc.pdf

Houtkooper, J. 2002. Arguing for an observational theory of psi. *Journal of Scientific Exploration*, *16*, 171–85. Available at: http://www.scientificexploration.org/journal/volume-16-number-2-2002

Schmidt, S. 2015. Experimental research on distant intention phenomena. In E. Cardeña, J. Palmer, and D. Marcusson-Clavertz (Eds) *Parapsychology: A Handbook for the 21st Century*. Jefferson, N.C., McFarland.

Chapter 12: Conclusion: Parapsychology's value

Hövelmann, G. 2015. On the usefulness of parapsychology for science at large. In Cardeña, E., Palmer, J., and Marcusson-Clavertz, D. (Eds) 2015. *Parapsychology: A Handbook for the 21st Century*. Jefferson, NC, McFarland.

Wagenmakers, E.J., Wetzels, R., Borsboom, D., Kievit, R., and van der Maas, H.L.J. 2015. A skeptical eye on psi. In E. May and S. Marwaha (Eds) *Extrasensory Perception: Support, Skepticism, and Science.* ABC-CLIO.

Watt, C. and Kennedy, J.E. 2015. Lessons from the first two years of operating a study registry. *Frontiers in Psychology, 6,* 173. Available at: http://journal.frontiersin.org/article/10.3389/fpsyg.2015.00173/full

Additional recommended readings

Cardeña, E., Lynn, S.J., and Krippner, S. (Eds) 2014. *Varieties of Anomalous Experience: Examining the Scientific Evidence,* 2nd ed. Washington, DC, American Psychological Association.

Cardeña, E., Palmer, J. and Marcusson-Clavertz, D. (Eds) 2015. *Parapsychology: A Handbook for the 21st Century.* Jefferson, NC, McFarland. (This handbook picks up from where Wolman's handbook, below, ends.)

Irwin, H.J. and Watt, C. 2007. *An Introduction to Parapsychology,* 5th ed. Jefferson, NC, McFarland.

Kurtz, P. (Ed.) 1985. *A Skeptic's Handbook of Parapsychology.* Buffalo, NY, Prometheus.

May, E. and Marwaha, S. (Eds) 2015. *Extrasensory Perception: Support, Skepticism, and Science.* ABC-CLIO. (This handbook has more emphasis on theoretical matters than Cardeña's '21st Century' handbook.)

Wolman, B.B. (Ed.) (1977). *Handbook of Parapsychology.* New York, Van Nostrand Reinhold.

Online resources

The University of Edinburgh's Online Parapsychology Course, and Koestler Parapsychology Unit website: https://koestlerunit.wordpress.com/

Parapsychological Association website: http://www.parapsych.org/

Society for Psychical Research website: http://www.spr.ac.uk/

The Committee for Skeptical Inquiry website: http://www.csicop.org/

Glossary

Here is an explanation of some terms used in this book. Frequently encountered terms are also explained in more detail at the beginning of the book.

Bio-PK: Mental influence over biological systems, including plants, insects and animals, in vitro samples, and humans. This category of research includes remote staring detection and distant healing.

Clairvoyance: The obtaining of information about a place or event by unknown means (from the French words *clair*, meaning 'clear', and *voyance*, meaning 'vision').

Experient: A person reporting a paranormal experience.

Experimenter effect: The influence of the experimenter upon the behaviour of the participant or the outcome of the study. In psychology, this usually refers to ways in which the experimenter inadvertently communicates their expectations to the participant. In parapsychology, this may additionally refer to the possibility that the experimenter is using their putative psychic abilities directly to obtain the desired outcome.

Extrasensory perception (ESP): The ability to obtain information without the use of the known senses or inference. Subcategories are telepathy, precognition, and clairvoyance.

fMRI: Functional magnetic resonance imaging – a procedure that uses changes in brain blood flow to obtain an image of brain function.

Ganzfeld: A method that parapsychologists use to test for ESP. Deriving originally from Gestalt psychology, it involves placing the participant in an unpatterned sensory environment (usually involving physical relaxation, red light, and the sound of white noise).

Macro-PK: The movement of physical objects with the mind, visible to the naked eye, sometimes referred to as 'telekinesis'.

Medium: A person who claims to be able to communicate with the deceased.

Meta-analysis: A statistical method to combine the results of a group of similar studies and examine any patterns therein.

Micro-PK: Mental influence over small-scale physical systems, such as dice and random number generators (RNGs), only detectable using statistics.

NDE: Near-death experience – reported memories of emotions, thoughts, and perceptions associated with a period of unconsciousness (can occur without actual physical proximity to death).

OBE: Out-of-body experience – the sensation that one has left one's physical body.

Participant: A person who volunteers to take part in experimental research, usually in a laboratory (previously referred to as the 'subject').

Placebo: The Latin for *I shall please*. A sham treatment given to patients, usually in a clinical trial, in order to measure the effects of the patient's expectancy on their reported symptoms. If the patient reports a change in symptoms after taking a sham treatment, this is known as a placebo response.

Precognition: The perception of information about future events, also referred to as premonition, future sight, second sight, and prophesy (from the Latin word *præ-*, meaning 'before', and *cognitio*, meaning 'acquiring knowledge').

Presentiment: The unconscious perception of future events or information. Measured indirectly, either through physiological measures, or through performance on cognitive or behavioural tasks.

Psi: (rhymes with 'eye') – a neutral umbrella term denoting the unknown factor underlying both ESP and PK phenomena.

Psi-hitting: Psi task scoring that is significantly above mean chance expectation.

Psi-missing: Psi task scoring that is significantly below mean chance expectation.

Psychokinesis (PK): The influence of mind on an object, physical system, or biological system, without physical interaction (from the Greek ψυχή or *psyche*, meaning 'mind', and κίνησις, meaning 'movement'). Abbreviated as PK; subcategories are Macro-PK, Micro-PK, and Bio-PK.

QRPs: Questionable research practices – decisions made by a researcher that may undermine the validity of the reported findings (e.g. conducting multiple statistical analyses but only reporting the analysis that supported the hypothesis).

Remote staring detection: A person detecting when they are being stared at by another person with whom they have no sensory contact. Parapsychologists first studied this by asking the 'staree' to guess when they were being stared at, but later turned to non-verbal or unconscious measures of staring detection, such as physiological activation.

RNG: Random number generator (or random event generator, REG) – apparatus that generates a random sequence of digits (e.g. 1s or 0s). Usually either based on unpredictable processes such as radioactive decay (a 'live' or 'true' RNG) or a mathematical algorithm (a 'pseudo-RNG').

Séance: A gathering of people, usually in the dark and in the presence of a medium, with the intention of communication with a deceased person.

Sitter: A person who visits a medium.

Study registration: Making a statement (often public) of the planned method, hypotheses, and analyses for a study before any data has been conducted.

Super-ESP: The hypothesis that mediums, rather than obtaining information from the deceased, are actually using ESP to obtain information from the living, or clairvoyance to obtain information from the environment, even if those present at the séance are unaware of this information. Generally regarded as more parsimonious than the survival hypothesis.

Survival: The hypothesis that some aspect of (usually) human personality, character, or memory, survives physical death.

Telepathy: The transfer of information between individuals by means other than the known senses (from the Greek τῆλε or *tele*, meaning 'distant', and πάθος or *pathos*, meaning 'feeling').

Index